Dedicated to my parents, Dr. Joel Recinos and Andrea Diederich. I thank God that He chose you guys to raise me, and my lesser-talented siblings.

Also to my wonderful wife, Jackie, who has been my rock through years of marital bliss; and to our three amazing children, who shall remain nameless and gender nonspecific in view of internet predators and/or fraud by social engineering.

And lastly to James Newton-King, author of Json.NET. He invented an awesome piece of software and gave it away free to a grateful software community, asking nothing in return. A very noble act, if you ask me.

Json.NET Declassified

by

Joel Recinos

Computer Programmer

Table of Contents

{

"Chapter" : "One",

"Title" : "Introduction to Json.NET"

}

Websites today are no longer stand-alone applications where all the content is pulled from a local database. Gone are the days when exchanging data with a third-party company mean importing a flat-file database, a CSV file, or an XML file.

Today's web sites enhance utility by sharing data through web services. Businesses exchange data over the internet on a daily basis; both by providing an API to clients and business partners, and also by consuming external APIs from vendors and third-parties. This exchange of data allows businesses to keep clients informed of products and orders status, share sales data with business partners, and inventory data with vendors. Small web sites enhance their content by consuming data from third-party web services for movies, news feeds, Facebook and Twitter posts. E-commerce web sites consume and display real-time shipping rates from

UPS and FedEx API, and process credit card payments by calling Cybersource or Braintree API.

Not long ago, XML was king. Web services returned XML, or used a SOAP based XML format. But gradually JSON made inroads, mostly by being easier to parse and having a smaller data size to transmit over the internet. (The JSON vs. XML topic, and which is better, is still hotly debated and covered in greater detail on numerous web sites, so documenting its arguments here are beyond the scope of this book.)

JSON has become the predominate data exchange format. Companies today that were around in the old days may still offer their API in both XML and JSON format, while newer companies with limited resources may choose to only develop a JSON API. In any event, JSON is everywhere. If you are a software developer, sooner or later, you will be asked to work with JSON.

This is where Json.NET comes in. Originally created in 2006 by James Newton-King, a then 22 year-old software developer out of New Zealand, as a handy way to escape JSON strings, Json.NET has evolved over time to become a robust, feature-rich and comprehensive library. With over fifteen million downloads of the Json.NET library and growing, it is arguably the best JSON serializer for .NET! Even Microsoft chose to use it as their default serializer for WebApi! And it is free under the least restrictive open source MIT license! J.N.K. has unselfishly given a valuable free gift to the software developing community and yet we didn't get him a thing.

But because of the phenomenal growth of the Json.NET library, there is a bit of a learning curve to using it effectively; especially considering it seems like there are multiple ways of achieving the same results using different Json.NET classes and methods. This can be very confusing for first-time users, as reflected by the thousands of Json.NET questions posted on StackOverflow.com. These questions arise because, although the online documentation provided by Json.NET's author is amazingly comprehensive and thorough, it can be overwhelming for first-time users. Unfortunately, the documentation is not in any kind of sequential order for someone looking to start at the very beginning and learn basic concepts before tackling the more advanced features. That's why I wrote this book, to serve as a guide and save you some time and frustration spent on trial and error.

The main Json.NET namespaces are:

Newtonsoft.Json;

Newtonsoft.Json.Bson;

Newtonsoft.Json.Converters;

Newtonsoft.Json.Linq;

Newtonsoft.Json.Linq.JsonPath;

Newtonsoft.Json.Schema;

Newtonsoft.Json.Serialization;

Newtonsoft.Json.Utilities;

Installing Json.NET

I will not go into much detail here about installing Json.NET. I am going to assume that a dynamic C# guru such as yourself can figure it out. However, if you are really a glutton for nitty-gritty details, you can take a gander at the info in Appendix A.

Who is this book for?

This book is for experienced C# developers with little day-to-day experience with Json.NET. It assumes you are already familiar with C# development and Visual Studio. If you are running ASP.NET Core in a Linux environment, or doing mobile development, you may have to make a few tweaks to the code samples here and there, but the basic concepts remain the same.

All sample code can be found at: github.com/JsonNetDeclassified/Code

Enough jibber-jabber! If you are ready to serialize some JSON using Json.NET, then read on, Garth!

{

"Chapter" : "Two",

"Title" : "JsonConvert Class"

}

JsonConvert is probably the class you will use the most when converting a C# class to a JSON string (serialize) or converting a JSON string to a C# class (deserialize). It helps to remember the difference between the two by focusing on the letter "S": (S)erialize returns a (S)tring. Therefore, deserialize will return the other, a class object. JsonConvert is a static class with static methods, so you need not create an instance to call its methods.

The JsonConvert class has two main methods; SerializeObject() and DeserializeObject(). The class also contains variations of these methods for working with XML and async versions that were since deprecated by .NET's Task classes. The Serialize/Deserialize methods are easy to use. You simply pass them the object you want to serialize, or the string you want to deserialize.

The DeserializeObject() method allows you to specify the type of object to return by specifying generic type parameters in the diamond brackets <>, such as DeserializeObject<Product>(jsonStr). If you do not specify a return type, the method returns an object instance, which holds either a JObject or JArray object, depending on whether the source JSON is an object or an array. A JSON object is denoted by curly braces: {}. An array is denoted by square brackets: []. The DeserializeObject() method has a couple overloads which allow you to pass in a JsonSerializerSettings object or a JsonConverter, which are discussed in later chapters. The SerializeObject() method also has several overloads to accept various parameter combinations for specifying type and formatting, as well as JsonSerializerSettings and JsonConverter.

SerializeObject() and DeserializeObject() methods

Let's debug some short C# examples to further illustrate this point. Fire up Visual Studio and create a console project. Add a reference to the Newtonsoft.Json.dll to your project. Whenever I dabble in a console project, I prefer to avoid having to create new static methods in program.cs. Therefore, I like to add a new Class1.cs file to the project. Then, in the main() function of program.cs, I can simply create a Class1 object and call a method, as shown in figure 2-1.

```
Figure 2-1

class Program
{
    static void Main(string[] args)
    {
        var class1 = new Class1();
        class1.Go();
    }
}
```

I create a public Go() method in Class1 and enter the code shown in figure 2-2. I have kept all the code samples fairly small, just enough to demonstrate the point without having to type huge code blocks. I, for one, learn faster by typing in the code as opposed to copying and pasting code. In any event, all sample code can be found at: **github.com/JsonNetDeclassified/Code**. Set a break point on the Go() method so you can step-thru it during debug to peek at the variables. Also add a using directive: using Newtonsoft.Json;

```
Figure 2-2

class Class1
{
    public void Go()
    {
        var prodObj = new Product() { Name = "Shirt" };
        var jsonStr = JsonConvert.SerializeObject(prodObj);

        var newObj = JsonConvert.DeserializeObject(jsonStr);
        var typeName = newObj.GetType().Name;
    }
}

public class Product
{
    public String Name { get; set; }
}
```

In the above code box, we define a small Product class with a single property. We create a Product instance and assign it to the prodObj variable. Then we serialize that object to a JSON string using the SerializeObject() method and assign it to the jsonStr variable. If you debug this code in Visual Studio, hover over the jsonStr variable and choose the Text Visualizer. You can see the JSON contents: {"Name":"Shirt"}. The JSON is then passed to the DeserializeObject() method without specifying a return object type. The typeName variable will contain the value: JObject. This is consistent with the type returned with a JSON object source (as opposed to getting a JArray object if the JSON source begins and ends with square brackets).

It is important to note that the DeserializeObject() method will, by default, actually return an item of type "object" and not "JObject" or "JArray". So you might want to cast that back to JObject or JArray, as shown in figure 2-3, especially for IntelliSense purposes. Though if you do that, you will need to add a new using directive since the JObject class and the JArray class are in a different namespace: using Newtonsoft.Json.Linq;

```
Figure 2-3

var newObj = (JObject)JsonConvert.DeserializeObject(jsonStr);
```

Now let's see what happens when a JSON *array* is passed to the DeserializeObject() method without specifying a return type, as shown in figure 2-4.

```
Figure 2-4

class Class1
{
    public void Go()
    {
        var obj = new Product() { Name = "Shirt" };
        var pArray = new Product[] { obj };
        var jsonStr = JsonConvert.SerializeObject(pArray);

        var newObj = JsonConvert.DeserializeObject(jsonStr);
        var typeName = newObj.GetType().Name;
    }
}

public class Product
{
    public String Name { get; set; }
}
```

This time we assigned the product we created to a product array named pArray. When we pass the array to the SerializeObject() method, the jsonStr variable will contain: [{"Name":"Shirt"}]. Notice the beginning and ending square brackets, which denote a JSON array. When we pass this JSON string to the DeserializeObject() method without specifying a return type, the typeName variable will contain: JArray.

We would get the same result if we serialized a *list* of products instead of an array, as shown in figure 2-5.

```
Figure 2-5

var pList = new List<Product>() { prodObj };
```

We discuss working with JObject and JArray in a later chapter. So, for right now, it is better if we work with a strongly-typed object. For that, we must tell DeserializeObject() what kind of object we want returned.

```
Figure 2-6

class Class1
{
```

```
    public void Go()
    {
        var prodObj = new Product() { Name = "Shirt" };
        var jsonStr = JsonConvert.SerializeObject(prodObj);

        var newObj =
                    JsonConvert.DeserializeObject<Product>(jsonStr);
        var typeName = newObj.GetType().Name;
    }
}

public class Product
{
    public String Name { get; set; }
}
```

The only change we made to the code in figure 2-6 was adding "<Product>" to the DeserializeObject() method. Now the newObject variable will be of type Product and, of course, the typeName variable will contain: Product.

In Json.NET, you will discover that there are several ways to achieve the same result. In figure 2-3, we used an explicit cast back to JObject by specifying the cast type inside parenthesis. But you could also have used the <T> syntax like we did in figure 2-7.

```
Figure 2-7

var newObj = JsonConvert.DeserializeObject<JObject>(jsonStr);
```

It is important to note that you cannot explicitly cast JObject or JArray to a different custom class. This would throw an InvalidCastException and is sometimes unexpected by newbies. This is demonstrated in figure 2-8.

```
Figure 2-8

//this will fail
var newObj = (Product)JsonConvert.DeserializeObject(jsonStr);

//this will not
var newObj = JsonConvert.DeserializeObject<Product>(jsonStr);
```

I also wanted to show what happens when there is a collection property defined in the deserialization class. In this case, Json.NET will append to the collection any new values found in the JSON source. In the code displayed in figure 2-9, we modified our Product class to add a List of sizes and a constructor to initialize it with two sizes.

```
Figure 2-9

public class Product
{
    public String Name { get; set; }
    public List<String> Sizes { get; set; }

    //constructor initializes sizes list
    public Product()
    {
        Sizes = new List<string> { "Small", "Medium" };
    }
}

public class Class1
{
    public void Go()
    {
        //sample source JSON
        var jsonStr = @"{
            ""Name"": ""Shirt"",
            ""Sizes"": [""Large""]
        }";

        var newObj =
                    JsonConvert.DeserializeObject<Product>(jsonStr);
    }
}
```

Our sample JSON source contains a Name element and an additional size. If we were to serialize the newObj object to see what kind of data it contained, it would produce the following JSON:

{"Name":"Shirt","Sizes":["Small","Medium","Large"]}

As expected, newObj now contains three sizes instead of just the two from the constructor. Json.NET appends any new items in the JSON to an existing collection.

With just this little bit of knowledge gained, you are now equipped to consume and parse JSON from a third-party API. Let's try it!

We are going to fetch JSON from the Google Books API and parse it using Json.NET. Google Books contains a vast database on books and their authors. We use the Google Books API because, at the time of this writing, you can use their API without registering for an account or developer key. For clarity, I split the API url over two lines to avoid wrapping.

There are several ways to make an HTTP request in C#. For brevity, the code in figure 2-10 uses the HttpClient class. Therefore, you will need to add a reference for System.Net.Http dll to your project. You also need to add a using directive for:

using System.Net.Http;

```
Figure 2-10

public void Go()
{
    var jsonStr = string.Empty;
    var host = "https://www.googleapis.com";
    var url = host + "/books/v1/volumes?q=isbn:9780141314570";

    //first we make a call to the API
    using (var client = new HttpClient())
    {
        var response = client.GetAsync(url).Result;
        jsonStr = response.Content.ReadAsStringAsync().Result;
    }

    //deserialize the JSON to our Book class
    var book = JsonConvert.DeserializeObject<Book>(jsonStr);
    var bookName = book.items[0].volumeInfo.title;
}
```

The code in figure 2-10 starts by calling the Google Books API with a url containing the ISBN for the S.E. Hinton book: "The Outsiders". Figure 2-11 shows the JSON that was returned by the API and assigned to the jsonStr variable:

```
Figure 2-11

{
 "kind": "books#volumes",
 "totalItems": 1,
 "items": [
  {
   "kind": "books#volume",
   "id": "LOnpPwAACAAJ",
   "etag": "E9BpDKSgEMQ",
   "selfLink":
"https://www.googleapis.com/books/v1/volumes/LOnpPwAACAAJ",
   "volumeInfo": {
    "title": "The Outsiders",
    "authors": [
     "S. E. Hinton"
    ],
    "publisher": "Puffin HC",
    "publishedDate": "2002-06-27",
```

```
    "description": "The Socs's idea of having a good time is beating
up Greasers like Ponyboy, the rough, tough, long-haired kids from
the other side of town. Ponyboy knows what to expect and knows he
can count on his friends - until the night someone goes too far.",
    "industryIdentifiers": [
     {
      "type": "ISBN_10",
      "identifier": "0141314575"
     },
     {
      "type": "ISBN_13",
      "identifier": "9780141314570"
     }
    ],
    "readingModes": {
     "text": false,
     "image": false
    },
    "pageCount": 218,
    "printType": "BOOK",
    "categories": [
     "Alienation (Social psychology)"
    ],
    "averageRating": 4.0,
    "ratingsCount": 302,
    "maturityRating": "NOT_MATURE",
    "allowAnonLogging": false,
    "contentVersion": "preview-1.0.0",
    "imageLinks": {
     "smallThumbnail":
"http://books.google.com/books/content?id=LOnpPwAACAAJ&printsec=fron
tcover&img=1&zoom=5&source=gbs_api",
     "thumbnail":
"http://books.google.com/books/content?id=LOnpPwAACAAJ&printsec=fron
tcover&img=1&zoom=1&source=gbs_api"
    },
    "language": "en",
    "previewLink":
"http://books.google.com/books?id=LOnpPwAACAAJ&dq=isbn:9780141314570
&hl=&cd=1&source=gbs_api",
    "infoLink":
"http://books.google.com/books?id=LOnpPwAACAAJ&dq=isbn:9780141314570
&hl=&source=gbs_api",
    "canonicalVolumeLink":
"https://books.google.com/books/about/The_Outsiders.html?hl=&id=LOnp
PwAACAAJ"
   },
   "saleInfo": {
    "country": "US",
    "saleability": "NOT_FOR_SALE",
    "isEbook": false
   },
   "accessInfo": {
    "country": "US",
    "viewability": "NO_PAGES",
    "embeddable": false,
    "publicDomain": false,
    "textToSpeechPermission": "ALLOWED",
```

```
    "epub": {
     "isAvailable": false
    },
    "pdf": {
     "isAvailable": false
    },
    "webReaderLink":
"http://play.google.com/books/reader?id=LOnpPwAACAAJ&hl=&printsec=frontcover&source=gbs_api",
    "accessViewStatus": "NONE",
    "quoteSharingAllowed": false
   },
   "searchInfo": {
    "textSnippet": "The Socs&#39;s idea of having a good time is beating up Greasers like Ponyboy, the rough, tough, long-haired kids from the other side of town."
   }
  }
 ]
}
```

In order for Json.NET to deserialize the JSON to a strongly-typed object, we need to define a class to match the Google Books JSON. Luckily, Visual Studio makes this very easy. Simply copy the JSON to the clipboard, and click on a new line in the C# code where you want to define a new class. Select menu item: Edit -> Paste Special -> Paste JSON As Classes. Figure 2-12 shows the classes defined from pasting the JSON.

Figure 2-12

```
public class Rootobject
{
    public string kind { get; set; }
    public int totalItems { get; set; }
    public Item[] items { get; set; }
}

public class Item
{
    public string kind { get; set; }
    public string id { get; set; }
    public string etag { get; set; }
    public string selfLink { get; set; }
    public Volumeinfo volumeInfo { get; set; }
    public Saleinfo saleInfo { get; set; }
    public Accessinfo accessInfo { get; set; }
    public Searchinfo searchInfo { get; set; }
}

public class Volumeinfo
{
```

```
    public string title { get; set; }
    public string[] authors { get; set; }
    public string publisher { get; set; }
    public string publishedDate { get; set; }
    public string description { get; set; }
    public Industryidentifier[] industryIdentifiers { get; set; }
    public Readingmodes readingModes { get; set; }
    public int pageCount { get; set; }
    public string printType { get; set; }
    public string[] categories { get; set; }
    public float averageRating { get; set; }
    public int ratingsCount { get; set; }
    public string maturityRating { get; set; }
    public bool allowAnonLogging { get; set; }
    public string contentVersion { get; set; }
    public Imagelinks imageLinks { get; set; }
    public string language { get; set; }
    public string previewLink { get; set; }
    public string infoLink { get; set; }
    public string canonicalVolumeLink { get; set; }
}

public class Readingmodes
{
    public bool text { get; set; }
    public bool image { get; set; }
}

public class Imagelinks
{
    public string smallThumbnail { get; set; }
    public string thumbnail { get; set; }
}

public class Industryidentifier
{
    public string type { get; set; }
    public string identifier { get; set; }
}

public class Saleinfo
{
    public string country { get; set; }
    public string saleability { get; set; }
    public bool isEbook { get; set; }
}

public class Accessinfo
{
    public string country { get; set; }
    public string viewability { get; set; }
    public bool embeddable { get; set; }
    public bool publicDomain { get; set; }
    public string textToSpeechPermission { get; set; }
    public Epub epub { get; set; }
    public Pdf pdf { get; set; }
    public string webReaderLink { get; set; }
    public string accessViewStatus { get; set; }
```

```
    public bool quoteSharingAllowed { get; set; }
}

public class Epub
{
    public bool isAvailable { get; set; }
}

public class Pdf
{
    public bool isAvailable { get; set; }
}

public class Searchinfo
{
    public string textSnippet { get; set; }
}
```

Visual Studio does a pretty good job of creating a serialization class, but there are a couple things to watch out for. To begin with, “Rootobject” is not a very good name for the main class. Let’s change this to “Book”. Secondly, though this is not an issue with *our* JSON, but Visual Studio is not so good with re-using classes. It tends to define a new class for each nested property, even if they share identical class names and properties. Another issue is with data types. Visual Studio does its best to guess the data type based on the property value. This may be valid for one request, but another request may return a slightly different value for the property that may not match the previous data type. This can sometimes occur with arrays and numbers. We show you how to fix this in another chapter.

The code in figure 2-10 then calls the DeserializeObject<Book>(jsonStr) method, and extracts the book title from our strongly-typed object using dot notation. The bookName variable would now contain “The Outsiders”. A pretty powerful but simple way to exchange data with a third-party website.

The downside of this example is having to create numerous classes to deserialize the JSON. This approach is fine for calling an in-house API developed and maintained by your company. You will most likely be aware of any planned changes to the schema, and adjust your code accordingly. But what about a third-party API where you have no control over any schema changes, much less any advance warning? Adding or removing properties, or changing data types can break your application. In a later chapter we discuss how to work around these issues using JsonSerializerSettings, JsonConverters or doing partial serialization. But what if we don't want to add new classes to our code base every time we call a new third-party API? Maybe we just want to use one value from the API and ignore the rest of the data. For those reasons, we can use dynamic objects instead of a class, especially if we already know the names of the properties we want to use. Let's take another look at the code to see what changes need to be made.

```
Figire 2-13

public void Go()
{
    var jsonStr = string.Empty;
    var host = "https://www.googleapis.com";
    var url = host + "/books/v1/volumes?q=isbn:9780141314570";

    //first we make a call to the API
    using (var client = new HttpClient())
    {
        var response = client.GetAsync(url).Result;
        jsonStr = response.Content.ReadAsStringAsync().Result;
    }

    //deserialize the JSON to a dynamic object
    var book = JsonConvert.DeserializeObject<dynamic>(jsonStr);
    var bookName = book.items[0].volumeInfo.title.ToString();
}
```

The only change made to the code in figure 2-13 is with the last two lines. Instead of defining the generic type parameter of <Book>, we specified a dynamic type. A dynamic object doesn't change the type, but does allow you to specify whatever property names you wish without causing a compiler error. The compiler will know that the type and any methods or properties will not be known until runtime. This prevents compiler errors while saving you from having to define a strongly-typed class just to grab a few properties. Of course, the methods and properties better exist at runtime or your application will throw an exception! Especially if you use dot notation. The downside of using dynamic types is there is no IntelliSense. So you need to find out the correct spelling of all properties and methods beforehand to avoid runtime errors.

After deserialization is complete, we can then extract the book's title using dot notation. However, if you prefer using bracket notation, you can get the book's title using: (string)book["items"][0]["volumeInfo"]["title"]. Notice we had to explicitly cast the book title to a string. This is because the run-time object resolves to a JValue type, which is a class in the Newtonsoft.Json.Linq namespace that inherits from the JToken abstract class. JValue can hold many different data types (like string, float, boolean, integer to name a few) which makes casting to string necessary. We could also have used the JValue.Value property, which returns the underlying token value: var bookName = book.items[0].volumeInfo.title.Value; The JValue.Value property is of type "object" so it can hold all data types. Alternatively, we could have also used the ToObject() method defined in the JToken base class. The code would look like this: var bookName = book.items[0].volumeInfo.title.ToObject<string>();

DeserializeAnonymousType() method

Another way to avoid creating a class to deserialize third-party JSON, is to deserialize to an anonymous object using the DeserializeAnonymousType() method. Though to be fair, defining an anonymous type for complex JSON can become as tedious as defining numerous classes. An anonymous type is a type that doesn't have a name. The variable the anonymous object is assigned to has a name, but the type itself does not. Therefore you must use the var keyword when defining the variable, because there is no type name to use. The DeserializeAnonymousType() method provides the best of both worlds: no class to define while still retaining IntelliSense.

Figure 2-14 shows how the code would look when deserializing to an anonymous type:

```
Figure 2-14

public void Go()
{
    var jsonStr = string.Empty;
    var host = "https://www.googleapis.com";
    var url = host + "/books/v1/volumes?q=isbn:9780141314570";

    //first we make a call to the API
    using (var client = new HttpClient())
    {
        var response = client.GetAsync(url).Result;
        jsonStr = response.Content.ReadAsStringAsync().Result;
```

```
    }

    //deserialize JSON to an anonymous object of properties needed
    var Book = new
    {
        items = new[] {
            new {
                volumeInfo = new {
                    title = ""
                }
            }
        }
    };
    var book = JsonConvert.DeserializeAnonymousType(jsonStr, Book);
    var bookName = book.items[0].volumeInfo.title;
}
```

Notice how we created an anonymous object named Book with just the properties we needed. It would be quite tedious to create a property for every element in the JSON, especially if we did not intend to use them.

DeserializeObjectAsync() method

We will not go into the async versions of the Serialize/Deserialize methods since they are deprecated. You can instead use the .Net Task class. Figure 2-15 shows how the code would look using tasks. Don't forget to add a using directive: using System.Threading;

```
Figure 2-15

class Class1
{
    public void Go()
    {
        var task = GoTask();
        var prod = task.Result;
        var productName = prod.Name;
    }

    public async Task<Product> GoTask()
    {
        var prodObj = new Product() { Name = "Shirt" };
        var jsonStr = JsonConvert.SerializeObject(prodObj);

        return await
            Task.Factory.StartNew(() =>
            JsonConvert.DeserializeObject<Product>(jsonStr));
    }
}
```

```
public class Product
{
    public String Name { get; set; }
}
```

PopulateObject() method

The PopulateObject() method is handy for updating property values of an existing object with the values from another JSON object. For example, suppose you have a Product object with three properties for name, stock level and sizes. The three properties are used for display purposes on the product details page of an e-commerce website. Now suppose the product details controller calls an internal API prior to display to get updated stock levels and sizes. Let's start by adding the new properties to the Product class, as shown in figure 2-16.

```
Figure 2-16

public class Product
{
    public String Name { get; set; }
    public List<String> Sizes { get; set; }
    public int Stock { get; set; }
}
```

The list of strings for sizes will hold all available sizes for the product. Now for the PopulateObject() code. For the contrived example in figure 2-17, we initialize a product with one size. We did not define a stock level, so it will default to zero. If we were to serialize the prodObj object right after initialization, the JSON would look like this:

{"Name":"Shirt","Sizes":["Small"],"Stock":0}

```
Figure 2-17

class Class1
{
    public void Go()
    {
        var prodObj = new Product()
        {
            Name = "Shirt",
            Sizes = new List<string>() { "Small" }
        };
```

```
        var prodUpdateJson = GetProductInfo();

        JsonConvert.PopulateObject(prodUpdateJson, prodObj);
    }

    private string GetProductInfo()
    {
        //simulate JSON returned from API
        return @"
        {
            ""Sizes"": [""Medium"", ""Large""],
            ""Stock"":5
        }";
    }
}
```

Next, we retrieve our product update JSON by calling the GetProductInfo() method. This basic method simulates an API request and returns some simple product JSON, giving us a stock level of five, and a couple more sizes.

Finally we call the PopulateObject() method and pass it our existing object along with the product update JSON. Notice the method does not return a value. Json.NET works its magic behind the scenes and copies the values from one object to another. If we were to again serialize the prodObj object right after the call to PopulateObject(), the JSON would now reflect a new stock level of five, and two new sizes, in addition to the original size:

{"Name":"Shirt","Sizes":["Small","Medium","Large"],"Stock":5}.

SerializeXNode() and DeserializeXNode() method

The JsonConvert class also contains serialize/deserialize methods for working with XML. We will discuss these methods in detail later on in our chapter dedicated to XML processing.

{

"Chapter" : "Three",

"Title": "JsonSerializerSettings class"

}

The JsonSerializerSettings class contains many properties that are used to set options or preferences for the serialize/deserialize process. A JsonSerializerSettings object is usually initialized with the desired settings and then passed into a method as a parameter. Several of the Json.NET methods are overloaded to accept a JsonSerializerSettings object.

As shown in figure 3-1, a JsonSerializerSettings object is initialized, and then one or more properties are set. Notice that the values for these settings are actually enums, which makes it fairly easy to set them via IntelliSense. Finally, the JsonSerializerSettings object is passed as a method parameter, such as to the SerializeObject() method.

```
Figure 3-1

//instantiate an object and set the properties
var serializerSettings1 = new JsonSerializerSettings();
serializerSettings1.Formatting = Formatting.Indented;
serializerSettings1.NullValueHandling = NullValueHandling.Ignore;
```

```
//or use the object initializer syntax
var serializerSettings2 = new JsonSerializerSettings()
{
    Formatting = Formatting.Indented,
    NullValueHandling = NullValueHandling.Ignore
};

//pass the settings object as method parameter
var jsonStr = JsonConvert.SerializeObject(prodObj,
                                          serializerSettings2);
```

Let's take a look at the many settings provided and how to use them.

Formatting

If you've ever had a somewhat tech-savvy boss or co-worker ask you for a copy of the JSON posted to an API, you will appreciate the Formatting property. It is also useful if you ever have the need to display formatted JSON on a web page, as is sometimes needed in a password-protected admin page for editing purposes. In figure 3-2, we start by creating a familiar Product object. If we were to serialize this object directly after it has been instantiated, the object would produce the following JSON: .{"Name":"Shirt","Sizes":["Small"],"Stock":0}. But this one-line output is not very human-readable. Its as tricky as reading a sentence without spaces.

```
Figure 3-2

public void Go()
{
    var prodObj = new Product()
    {
        Name = "Shirt",
        Sizes = new List<string>() { "Small" }
    };

    var serializerSettings = new JsonSerializerSettings()
    {
        Formatting = Formatting.Indented
    };

    jsonStr = JsonConvert.SerializeObject(prodObj,
                    serializerSettings);
}
```

This is where the Formatting property comes in handy. We create a new JsonSerializerSettings object and assign it to a variable named serializerSettings. Inside, the Formatting property is initialized with the enum Formatting.Indented.

Finally, the serializerSettings object is passed to the SerializeObject() method. The beautifully-formatted JSON contents of the jsonStr variable appears in figure 3-3.

```
Figure 3-3

{
  "Name": "Shirt",
  "Sizes": [
    "Small"
  ],
  "Stock": 0
}
```

Actually, Json.NET makes outputting formatted JSON even easier by providing overloaded versions of the SerializeObject() and DeserializeObject() methods that directly accept Formatting.Indented as a parameter. So if all you're looking to do is quickly produce some formatted JSON, you don't have to go through the trouble of first creating a JsonSerializerSettings object, as in figure 3-4.

```
Figure 3-4

jsonStr = JsonConvert.SerializeObject(prodObj, Formatting.Indented);
```

NullValueHandling

It is quite common to fall victim to null values in JSON from third-party APIs, especially with data types that cannot contain null, such as int, double, etc. This will throw an exception and break your code. Most times it is not feasible to contact the third-party and ask them to remove the nulls in their JSON. That could take weeks. Most likely, your boss or customer will want this to be fixed right away. The good news is that it can quickly be resolved on your end using JsonSerializerSettings with a NullValueHandling property. For example, in figure 3-5, the GetProductJson() will simulate the product JSON returned from an external API. Notice the value for the Stock property contains null instead of an integer. When we try to deserialize this JSON to the Products class, it will throw an exception trying to convert null into an int.

```
Figure 3-5

public void Go()
{
    var jsonStr = GetProductJson();
    var newObj = JsonConvert.DeserializeObject<Product>(jsonStr);
}
```

```
private string GetProductJson()
{
    //simulate JSON returned from API
    return @"
    {
        ""Name"": ""Shirt"",
        ""Sizes"": [""Medium"", ""Large""],
        ""Stock"": null
    }";
}
```

What we really want to do is to ignore any null values and let the compiler initialize the corresponding object properties with a default value. In figure 3-6, we create a JsonSerializerSettings object and assign it to the settings variable. Then initialize the NullValueHandling property with the enum NullValueHandling.Ignore. Finally, the settings object is passed to the DeserializeObject() method.

```
Figure 3-6

public void Go()
{
    var jsonStr = GetProductJson();

    var settings = new JsonSerializerSettings()
    {
        NullValueHandling = NullValueHandling.Ignore
    };

    var newObj = JsonConvert.DeserializeObject<Product>(jsonStr,
                    settings);
}
```

This time, no exception is thrown. If we were to serialize newObj, the JSON would look like this: {"Name":"Shirt","Sizes":["Medium","Large"],"Stock":0}. Notice the Stock property now contains the default value of zero.

MissingMemberHandling

When using third-party APIs, new elements get added to the JSON all the time. By default, any members in the source JSON that are missing in the deserialization class are simply ignored. If you would like to be notified whenever the source JSON contains new elements that are missing from the deserialization class (not defined), you can set the MissingMemberHandling property of JsonSerializerSettings.

In figure 3-7, we modified our simulated JSON method GetProductJson() to return an extra UPC property that is not defined in the Product class.

```
Figure 3-7

public class Class3
{
    //WITHOUT MISSING MEMBER HANDLING
    public void Go()
    {
        var jStr = GetProductJson();
        var newObj = JsonConvert.DeserializeObject<Product>(jStr);
    }

    private string GetProductJson()
    {
        //simulate JSON returned from API
        return @"
        {
            ""Name"": ""Shirt"",
            ""Sizes"": [""Medium"", ""Large""],
            ""Stock"": 5,
            ""UPC"": ""123456789""
        }";
    }
}

//UPC property is missing from the class
public class Product
{
    public String Name { get; set; }
    public List<String> Sizes { get; set; }
    public int Stock { get; set; }
}
```

When we run this code, the newObj parameter would produce the following JSON when serialized: {"Name":"Shirt","Sizes":["Medium","Large"],"Stock":5}

Notice there is no UPC element. The code would run to completion without ever knowing the source JSON contained some new elements. In figure 3-8, we added a JsonSerializerSettings object and set the MissingMemberHandling property to enum MissingMemberHandling.Error. Then we pass the settings object as a parameter to the DeserializeObject() method.

```
Figure 3-8
public void Go()
{
    var jsonStr = GetProductJson();

    //WITH MISSING MEMBER HANDLING
    var settings = new JsonSerializerSettings()
    {
        MissingMemberHandling = MissingMemberHandling.Error
    };
```

```
    try
    {
        var newObj = JsonConvert.DeserializeObject<Product>(jsonStr,
                                    settings);
    }
    catch
    {
        //send notification
    }
}
```

Now when we run this code, Json.NET will detect that there are missing members in the class and throw a JsonSerializationException with the message: "Could not find member 'UPC' on object of type 'Product'. Path 'UPC'". Wrap the call inside a try/catch block and perform any necessary actions in the catch block, such as notifications or logging.

DateFormatHandling

The JSON spec does not define a standard format for date or time, probably because there is no date/time literal in JavaScript. So handling dates during serialization/deserialization can be a little tricky.

Currently, the default format used by Json.NET is the ISO 8601 format. But originally, Json.NET used the Microsoft Date Format ("\/Date(1198908717056)\/"). So if you need to maintain backwards compatibility for older versions of Json.NET, Microsoft Date Format is still supported.

Suppose we added a CreateDate property to our Product class, as in figure 3-9. We initialize a Product instance with a valid date. Then we create a JsonSerializerSettings object, setting the DateFormatHandling property to enum MicrosoftDateFormat, and pass it to the DeserializeObject() method as a parameter.

```
Figure 3-9

public class Product
{
    public String Name { get; set; }
    public List<String> Sizes { get; set; }
    public int Stock { get; set; }
    public DateTime CreateDate { get; set; }
}
```

```
public class Class1
{
    public void Go()
    {
        var prod = new Product()
        {
            Name = "Shirt",
            Sizes = new List<string>() { "Small" },
            CreateDate = DateTime.Parse("12/31/2018 09:22:45")
        };

        var settings = new JsonSerializerSettings()
        {
            DateFormatHandling =
                    DateFormatHandling.MicrosoftDateFormat
        };

        var jsonStr = JsonConvert.SerializeObject(prod, settings);
    }
}
```

When we call the SerializeObject() method, the jsonStr variable now contains:

{"Name":"Shirt","Sizes":["Small"],"Stock":0,"CreateDate":"\/Date(1546276965000-0800)\/"}

Notice the CreateDate value "\/Date(1546276965000-0800)\/" is in Microsoft Date Format. If we change the enum of DateFormatHandling to IsoDateFormat, the value of CreateDate would become: "2018-12-31T09:22:45".

Of course, there are a number of different date formats you will come across in third-party JSON. Fortunately, Json.NET has a more robust solution for dealing with reading and writing different date formats: JsonConverters. We discuss how in a later chapter on JsonConverters.

DefaultValueHandling

DefaultValueHandling determines whether properties that contain default values are written to the JSON or deserialized to a class. Default values in C# are null (strings and objects), false (booleans), 0 (integers, decimals, floats). You can also define a custom default value by decorating a class property with the .NET DefaultValueAttribute attribute. When doing so, it is important to understand that using the DefaultValueAttribute does not initialize the member with a default value. You still have to set its value in the code. Its use is mainly by form designers and code generators. However, Json.NET honors the DefaultValueAttribute during serializing/deserializing when used in conjunction with the DefaultValueHandling property.

The DefaultValueHandling enum contains four values: Include, Ignore, Populate, IgnoreAndPopulate. "Include" means all properties with default values will be written to the JSON (no effect when deserializing). "Ignore" means any properties containing default values will NOT be written to the JSON. "Populate" means properties not in the JSON will be set to their default value when deserializing. "IgnoreAndPopulate" works like Ignore when serializing and Populate when deserializing.

Don't forget to add this using directive: using System.ComponentModel;

DefaultValueHandling.Ignore

Let's take a look at the code in figure 3-10. Notice in the Product class we have added a DefaultValueAttribute to the CreateDate property, along with a specific DateTime value. This does not assign a value to the CreateDate property. It merely indicates which value is to be *considered* a default value. We assign the value for CreateDate in the Product object initializer. Notice we assign CreateDate a value we designated as a default value. Also notice the object initializer does not set a value for the stock property. Therefore, it will end up with the default value of zero. So, effectively, two properties, Stock and CreateDate, will be initialized with default values.

```
Figure 3-10

public class Product
{
    public String Name { get; set; }
    public List<String> Sizes { get; set; }
    public int Stock { get; set; }
    [DefaultValueAttribute(typeof(DateTime), "12/31/2018 09:22:45")]
    public DateTime CreateDate { get; set; }
}

public class Class1
{
    public void Go()
    {
        var prodObj = new Product()
        {
            Name = "Shirt",
            Sizes = new List<string>() { "Small" },
```

```
            CreateDate = DateTime.Parse("12/31/2018 09:22:45")
        };

        var jsonStrBefore = JsonConvert.SerializeObject(prodObj);

        var settings = new JsonSerializerSettings()
        {
            DefaultValueHandling = DefaultValueHandling.Ignore
        };

        var jsonStr =
                JsonConvert.SerializeObject(prodObj, settings);
    }
}
```

After Product instantiation, we serialize the prodObj object to the jsonStrBefore variable so that we can see what the JSON would look like before applying the DefaultValueHandling settings:

{"Name":"Shirt","Sizes":["Small"],"Stock":0,"CreateDate":"2018-12-31T09:22:45"}

As expected, Stock has the default value of 0, and CreateDate contains the default value we specified in the DefaultValueAttribute.

Next, a JsonSerializerSettings object is created with DefaultValueHandling set to DefaultValueHandling.Ignore. This time, when we pass the JsonSerializerSettings object to the SerializeObject() method, the JSON is considerably smaller:

{"Name":"Shirt","Sizes":["Small"]}

Notice the two properties with default values, Stock and CreateDate, were ignored and not written to the JSON.

DefaultValueHandling.Populate

Now let's try deserializing with DefaultValueHandling.Populate. The Product class in figure 3-11 has two properties decorated with DefaultValueAttribute: Stock and CreateDate. The attribute indicates which values are to be *considered* default values. The source JSON defined in the prodStr variable of the Go() method only contains values for the Name and Sizes properties, leaving Stock and CreateDate to be initialized with the .NET default values of 0 and 0/0/1901, respectively.

```
Figure 3-11

public class Product
{
    public String Name { get; set; }
    public List<String> Sizes { get; set; }
    [DefaultValueAttribute(5)]
    public int Stock { get; set; }
    [DefaultValueAttribute(typeof(DateTime), "12/31/2018 09:22:45")]
    public DateTime CreateDate { get; set; }
}

public class Class1
{
    public void Go()
    {
        var prodStr = "{\"Name\":\"Shirt\",\"Sizes\":[\"Small\"]}";

        var prodObjBefore =
                JsonConvert.DeserializeObject<Product>(prodStr);

        var settings = new JsonSerializerSettings()
        {
            DefaultValueHandling = DefaultValueHandling.Populate
        };

        var prdObj = JsonConvert.DeserializeObject<Product>(prodStr,
                                        settings);
    }
}
```

For comparison purposes we deserialize the JSON to prodObjBefore just to see the property values. As expected, the DefaultValueAttribute does not initialize members with values. Therefore, Stock and CreateDate contain the .NET default values, since none were specified in the source JSON.

```
prodObjBefore:
    Name        = "Shirt"
    Sizes       = Count = 1
    Stock       = 0
    CreateDate  = {1/1/0001 12:00:00 AM}
```

Next, a JsonSerializerSettings object is created with DefaultValueHandling set to the DefaultValueHandling.Populate enum. This time, when we pass the JsonSerializerSettings object to the DeserializeObject() method, the default values defined in the DefaultValueAttribute are finally honored in Stock and CreateDate:

```
prodObj:
    Name        = "Shirt"
    Sizes       = Count = 1
    Stock       = 5
    CreateDate  = {12/31/2018 9:22:45 AM}
```

ObjectCreationHandling

ObjectCreationHandling determines how objects created during deserialization are handled. From our previous deserialization examples, we've learned that Json.NET, by default, sets class properties with values retrieved from the JSON. Or in the case of the Product sizes collection, appends any new values found. But what if you don't want to append values from the source JSON to the collection? What if you want to replace the existing values with the new values found in the source JSON? This is where ObjectCreationHandling comes in handy.

Let's go back to our Product.Sizes deserialization example in figure 2-9. If you recall, our deserialization Product class had a constructor that initialized the sizes List<T> with two values. The source JSON contained an additional size. When the JSON was deserialized to a Product object, the sizes list contained all three sizes.

Let's revisit that code and alter the default outcome using ObjectCreationHandling. Instead of appending the new values to the sizes collection, let's replace them with the values from the source JSON. In figure 3-12, the source JSON defined in the jsonStr variable of the Go() method contains two different sizes than the two values initialized in the Product class constructor. Next, the code creates a JsonSerializerSettings object with ObjectCreationHandling set to Replace.

```
Figure 3-12

public class Product
{
    public String Name { get; set; }
    public List<String> Sizes { get; set; }

    //constructor populates sizes list
    public Product()
    {
        Sizes = new List<string> { "Small", "Medium" };
    }
}
```

```
public class Class1
{
    public void Go()
    {
        //sample source JSON
        var jsonStr = @"{
            ""Name"": ""Shirt"",
            ""Sizes"": [""Large"", ""X-Large""]
        }";

        var settings = new JsonSerializerSettings()
        {
            ObjectCreationHandling = ObjectCreationHandling.Replace
        };

        var newObj = JsonConvert.DeserializeObject<Product>(jsonStr,
                                settings);
    }
```

The settings object is passed to the DeserializeObject() method. If we were to serialize the newObj object, the JSON would look like this:

{"Name":"Shirt","Sizes":["Large","X-Large"]}

Notice the two size values initialized by the constructor were replaced by the values from the JSON, instead of Json.NET appending the new values to the existing collection.

ReferenceLoopHandling

ReferenceLoopHandling determines how reference loops are handled during serialization. For example, a class has a property with the same data type as the containing class. Any child object assigned to it might contain a reference back to the same object being serialized, creating a loop reference. Sound confusing? For example, suppose we want to add a new property to our Product class to hold a reference to a similar product a user might also be interested in. The new property is called Recommendations and set to a type of Product, as shown in figure 3-13.

```
Figure 3-13

public class Product
{
    public String Name { get; set; }
    public List<String> Sizes { get; set; }
    public Product Recommendations { get; set; }
}
```

The ReferenceLoopHandling enum has three items: Error, Ignore, Serialize. "Error" will throw an exception if it encounters a reference loop during serialization (which is the same thing that happens if you do not use any JsonSerializerSettings at all). "Ignore" will ignore skip any loop references and just not serialize the looped property to the JSON. "Serialize" will go ahead and serialize the loop references but this will most likely cause a stack overflow error at runtime if the object is nested indefinitely. Luckily, there is a work-around for that issue which we will discuss in a later chapter.

ReferenceLoopHandling.Error (same as not defining settings object)

In figure 3-14, we create two products and set each one as a recommendation to the other. An attempt to serialize either of the two products would throw a JsonSerializationException with the message "Self referencing loop detected for property 'Recommendations' with type 'Product'". The exception is thrown because prod2.Recommendations is set to prod1. Unfortunately, prod1.Recommendations is set back to prod2. Therefore, each product contains a nested reference to itself. This is a reference loop that will cause an exception during serialization.

```
Figure 3-14

public void Go()
{
    var prod1 = new Product()
    {
        Name = "Shirt",
        Sizes = new List<string>() { "Small" }
    };
    var prod2 = new Product()
    {
        Name = "Pants",
        Sizes = new List<string>() { "33" }
    };
    prod1.Recommendations = prod2;
    prod2.Recommendations = prod1;

    var jsonStr = JsonConvert.SerializeObject(prod2, settings);
}
```

ReferenceLoopHandling.Ignore

In figure 3-15, we added a JsonSerializerSettings object to the code with the ReferenceLoopHandling property set to Ignore.

```
Figure 3-15

public void Go()
{
    var prod1 = new Product()
    {
        Name = "Shirt",
        Sizes = new List<string>() { "Small" }
    };
    var prod2 = new Product()
    {
        Name = "Pants",
        Sizes = new List<string>() { "33" }
    };
    prod1.Recommendations = prod2;
    prod2.Recommendations = prod1;

    var settings = new JsonSerializerSettings()
    {
        ReferenceLoopHandling = ReferenceLoopHandling.Ignore
    };

    var jsonStr = JsonConvert.SerializeObject(prod2, settings);
}
```

This time the code runs smoothly. The contents of the jsonStr variable appear in Figure 3-16. Notice the JSON object value for Recommendations. It is a product object with the expected values for Name and Sizes. However, there is no Recommendations element in this product object. That is because it was a reference loop to the main object, so it has been ignored.

```
Figure 3-16

{
  "Name": "Pants",
  "Sizes": [
    "33"
  ],
  "Recommendations": {
    "Name": "Shirt",
    "Sizes": [
      "Small"
    ]
  }
}
```

ReferenceLoopHandling.Serialize

Let's go ahead try to serialize all loop references anyway. In figure 3-17, we set the ReferenceLoopHandling property to Serialize. This will compile just fine but would, unfortunately, cause a stack overflow at runtime when it attempts to serialize the loop references. To prevent a stack overflow, we can add a setting for PreserveReferencesHandling and set it to Objects. This allows the code to preserve a reference instead of removing it.

```
Figure 3-17

public void Go()
{
    var prod1 = new Product()
    {
        Name = "Shirt",
        Sizes = new List<string>() { "Small" }
    };
    var prod2 = new Product()
    {
        Name = "Pants",
        Sizes = new List<string>() { "33" }
    };
    prod1.Recommendations = prod2;
    prod2.Recommendations = prod1;

    var settings = new JsonSerializerSettings()
    {
        ReferenceLoopHandling = ReferenceLoopHandling.Serialize,
        PreserveReferencesHandling =
                                PreserveReferencesHandling.Objects
    };

    var jsonStr = JsonConvert.SerializeObject(prod2, settings);
}
```

The contents of the jsonStr variable appear in Figure 3-18. Notice that the object for the main pants product has been assigned a unique $id of "1". Also notice the nested shirt product object in the Recommendations element has been assigned a unique $id of "2". The important thing to notice is the Recommendations element of the nested shirt product. Instead of being removed entirely, as done in the previous example, it appears as a $ref object with a value of "1", which is a reference to the object with an $id of "1".

```
Figure 3-18

{
  "$id": "1",
  "Name": "Pants",
  "Sizes": [
    "33"
  ],
  "Recommendations": {
    "$id": "2",
```

```
    "Name": "Shirt",
    "Sizes": [
      "Small"
    ],
    "Recommendations": {
      "$ref": "1"
    }
  }
}
```

TypeNameHandling

TypeNameHandling allows you to embed the object's type information into the serialized JSON to ensure the same type is used during the deserialization process. Using the TypeNameHandling flag will add a $type property to the JSON. By default, Json.NET does not export any type information to the serialized JSON.

The code in figure 3-19 creates a JsonSerializerSettings object and sets the TypeNameHandling property to All. The settings object is then passed as a parameter to the SerializeObject() method.

```
Figure 3-19

public class Product
{
    public String Name { get; set; }
    public List<String> Sizes { get; set; }
    public int Stock { get; set; }
}

public class Class1
{
    public void Go()
    {
        var prodObj = new Product()
        {
            Name = "Shirt",
            Sizes = new List<string>() { "Small" }
        };

        var settings = new JsonSerializerSettings()
        {
            TypeNameHandling = TypeNameHandling.All
        };

        var jsonStr =
                JsonConvert.SerializeObject(prodObj, settings);
    }
}
```

The contents of the jsonStr variable after serialization are shown in figure 3-20. Notice the $type information for the root property contains the namespace and class name (the full name), along with a partial assembly name. The $type element in the sizes collection also displays the .NET information for class and partial assembly name. Notice the Sizes object also contains a $values object with the size values.

```
Figure 3-20

{
  "$type": "JsonNetTest.Product, JsonNetTest",
  "Name": "Shirt",
  "Sizes": {
    "$type": "System.Collections.Generic.List`1[[System.String,
               mscorlib]], mscorlib",
    "$values": [
      "Small"
    ]
  },
  "Stock": 0
}
```

TypeNameAssemblyFormat

If you wanted to add version information to the partial assembly name, you could then deserialize the source JSON to a specific version of the object. Let's add the TypeNameAssemblyFormat flag and set it to Full, as shown in figure 3-21. Don't forget to add a using directive for:

using System.Runtime.Serialization.Formatters;

```
Figure 3-21

public void Go()
{
    var prodObj = new Product()
    {
        Name = "Shirt",
        Sizes = new List<string>() { "Small" }
    };

    var settings = new JsonSerializerSettings()
    {
        TypeNameHandling = TypeNameHandling.All,
        TypeNameAssemblyFormat = FormatterAssemblyStyle.Full
    };

    var jsonStr = JsonConvert.SerializeObject(prodObj, settings);
}
```

The new contents of the jsonStr variable are shown in figure 3-22. This time, both $type elements also contain the version information.

```
Figure 3-22

{
  "$type": "JsonNetTest.Product, JsonNetTest, Version=1.0.0.0,
        Culture=neutral, PublicKeyToken=null",
  "Name": "Shirt",
  "Sizes": {
    "$type": "System.Collections.Generic.List`1[[System.String,
         mscorlib, Version=4.0.0.0, Culture=neutral,
         PublicKeyToken=b77a5c561934e089]], mscorlib,
         Version=4.0.0.0, Culture=neutral,
         PublicKeyToken=b77a5c561934e089",
    "$values": [
      "Small"
    ]
  },
  "Stock": 0,
  "Recommendations": null
}
```

TypeNameHandling.Arrays & TypeNameHandling.Auto

If you wanted to export $type information to the JSON for just the arrays, set TypeNameHandling to TypeNameHandling.Arrays.

Setting the value to TypeNameHandling.Auto ensures Json.NET will check whether the object matches its declared property and only writes the $type element to the JSON if they are not the same.

Now let's do the opposite. Let's deserialize JSON that contains a $type element back to the object type defined in the $type element. The JSON string defined in figure 3-23, contains the Product type information in the $type property. The Sizes object also contains a $type property with generic list info. We must still define a JsonSerializerSettings object with a TypeNameHandling setting, otherwise Json.NET will not know what to do with the $type property and will treat it as just another JSON item to be deserialized to the object.

Notice we are not using the generic version of the DeserializeObject() method. Ordinarily, using the regular DeserializeObject() method as we are, would return a JObject because we have not specified anywhere to deserialize to the Product class.

But because the Product class information is contained in the JSON in the $type element, Json.NET will know to deserialize the JSON into a Product instance.

When the code in figure 3-23 is run, Json.NET will read the class information contained in the $type property and deserialize the JSON to a Product object. If you hover over the objType variable during debugging, it will contain "Product" because obj is a Product instance instead of a regular JObject.

```
Figure 3-23

public void Go()
{
    var jsonStr = @"{
            ""$type"": ""JsonNetTest.Product, JsonNetTest"",
            ""Name"": ""Shirt"",
            ""Sizes"": {
               ""$type"": ""System.Collections.Generic.List`1[[
                             System.String, mscorlib]], mscorlib"",
               ""$values"": [
                ""Small""
               ]
            },
            ""Stock"": 0
    }";

    var settings = new JsonSerializerSettings
    {
        TypeNameHandling = TypeNameHandling.All
    };

    var obj = JsonConvert.DeserializeObject(jsonStr, settings);
    var objType = obj.GetType().Name;
}
```

MetadataPropertyHandling

The MetadataPropertyHandling setting works in conjunction with the TypeNameHandling setting when deserializing JSON that contains a $type property. Notice in figure 3-23 that the $type property is the first item in the object's root level. Json.NET expects any $type property to be the first item. If it is not, Json.NET will treat it as a regular property to be deserialized to the object.

This is where using the MetadataPropertyHandling setting comes in handy. If the source JSON, for some reason, has the properties out of order, and the $type property is not the first item listed, MetadataPropertyHandling can be set to instruct Json.NET to compensate for that by making two passes. The first pass would be to read through the entire JSON, looking for any $type property information. Of course, making two passes is slower, so there is a trade-off.

The code in figure 3-24 demonstrates what happens if the $type property is not first and we do not use the MetadataPropertyHandling property. Notice in the JSON string that Name is the first property listed. Even though we still specify the TypeNameHandling setting, Json.NET treats the $type property as a regular item and deserializes it to the obj object, giving it four properties instead of three. If you hover of the objType variable, it would read "JObject" instead of Product because Json.NET did not find the $type information in the JSON because it was not the first item listed. Consequently, the regular version of the DeserializeObject() returns a JObject.

```
Figure 3-24

public void Go()
{
    var jsonStr = @"{
                ""Name"": ""Shirt"",
                ""$type"": ""JsonNetTest.Product, JsonNetTest"",
                ""Sizes"": {
                    ""$type"": ""System.Collections.Generic.List`1[[
                                   System.String, mscorlib]], mscorlib"",
                    ""$values"": [
                        ""Small""
                    ]
                },
                ""Stock"": 0
    }";

    var settings = new JsonSerializerSettings
    {
        TypeNameHandling = TypeNameHandling.All
    };

    var obj = JsonConvert.DeserializeObject(jsonStr, settings);
    var objType = obj.GetType().Name;
}
```

In figure 3-25, we also add the MetadataPropertyHandling property to JsonSerializerSettings object and set it to ReadAhead. Now the $type property does not have to be listed first. So when the code runs this time, Json.NET will find the $type property and properly deserialize the JSON to a Product instance. If you hover over the objType variable, it contains "Product".

```
Figure 3-25

public void Go()
{
    var jsonStr = @"{
            ""Name"": ""Shirt"",
            ""$type"": ""JsonNetTest.Product, JsonNetTest"",
            ""Sizes"": {
            ""$type"": ""System.Collections.Generic.List`1[[
            "               System.String, mscorlib]], mscorlib"",
            ""$values"": [
                ""Small""
            ]
            },
            ""Stock"": 0
    }";

    var settings = new JsonSerializerSettings
    {
        TypeNameHandling = TypeNameHandling.All,
        MetadataPropertyHandling = MetadataPropertyHandling.ReadAhead
    };

    var obj = JsonConvert.DeserializeObject(jsonStr, settings);
    var objType = obj.GetType().Name;
}
```

Since obj is now a Product object, you can hover over it during debug and it would display the data in figure 3-26.

```
Figure 3-26

obj:
    Name        = "Shirt"
    Sizes       = Count = 1
    Stock       = 0
```

There is an important consideration when serializing type information into the JSON. If you are serializing and deserializing within the same assembly (application) there is no problem. But if you serialize assembly and namespace information into the JSON and then try to deserialize it with a new application with different assembly and namespace, it will fail. We discuss ways to deal with this in chapter twelve.

Converters

We will discuss JsonConverters at-length in later chapter, so we will not go into much detail here. What we want to point out in this section, is to be aware that after you learn how to create and use JsonConverters, you can embed a list of them inside a JsonSerializerSettings object, along with your other settings, and pass it to the serialization/deserialization process. The code for doing this is listed in figure 3-27. Don't forget to add a using directive for: using Newtonsoft.Json.Converters;

```
Figure 3-27

public void Go()
{
    var prodObj = new Product()
    {
        Name = "Shirt",
        Sizes = new List<string>() { "Small" }
    };

    var settings = new JsonSerializerSettings()
    {
        Converters = new List<JsonConverter>()
        {
            new JavaScriptDateTimeConverter()
        },
        ReferenceLoopHandling = ReferenceLoopHandling.Serialize
    };

    var jsonStr = JsonConvert.SerializeObject(prodObj, settings);
}
```

MemoryTraceWriter

MemoryTraceWriter is used by Json.NET to write log messages during the serialization/deserialization process. We go into much more detail about TraceWriter later on in the chapter about logging. So for right now, just be aware that you can enable logging messages using the default TraceWriter by creating and assigning a MemoryTraceWriter object to the TraceWriter property, as shown in the code in figure 3-28. You can view the log messages by peeking at the log variable. You will need to add a using directive for: using Newtonsoft.Json.Serialization;

```
Figure 3-28

public void Go()
{
    var traceWriter = new MemoryTraceWriter();

    var settings = new JsonSerializerSettings()
    {
        TraceWriter = traceWriter
    };
```

```
    var prod =
            JsonConvert.DeserializeObject<Product>(json, settings);
    var log = traceWriter.ToString();
}
```

Error Handling

If you recall, setting MissingMemberHandling to the Error enum would cause an exception to be thrown if an item in the JSON was missing from the deserialization class. Well, what if we wanted to know when such errors occurred, but we didn't want our program interrupted by an exception? JsonSerializerSettings provides an Error setting for just such graceful error handling.

In the code in figure 3-29, we first define a JSON string that contains a UPC item that is purposely not defined in the Product class. Next, we define a list of strings to hold all the error messages. Then we get down to defining the JsonSerializerSettings object. The first thing we do is set MissingMemberHandling to Error. That way, it will intentionally throw an exception because there is no UPC property defined in the Product class.

The second item we set in the JsonSerializerSettings object, is the Error property. Error is of type EventHandler so we must either assign it the name of a method to execute, or a delegate. A delegate is reference to a method that can be assigned to a variable and called indirectly. We'll look at using a delegate first, then we will cover the alternatives. We define an inline delegate anonymous method and assign it to the Error property. The delegate method will just add any error messages to the list of strings named error. It also sets the ErrorEventArgs Handled to true. If we don't set Handled to true, the exception thrown will disrupt the program. Don't forget to add a using directive for the ErrorEventArgs:

using Newtonsoft.Json.Serialization;

```
Figure 3-29

public void Go()
{
    var jStr = @"{
            ""Name"": ""Shirt"",
            ""Stock"": ""5"",
            ""Sizes"": [
                ""Large"",
                ""Medium""
```

```
            ],
            ""UPC"": ""123456789""
        }";

    var errors = new List<string>();
    var settings = new JsonSerializerSettings
    {
        MissingMemberHandling = MissingMemberHandling.Error,
        Error = delegate (object sender, ErrorEventArgs errorArgs)
        {
            errors.Add(errorArgs.ErrorContext.Error.Message);
            //mark error as handled or exception is thrown
            errorArgs.ErrorContext.Handled = true;
        }
    };

    var prod =
            JsonConvert.DeserializeObject<Product>(jStr, settings);

    if (errors.Any())
        log(String.Join(",", errors.ToArray()));
}
```

When the DeserializeObject() method is finally called, the error caused by UPC missing from the Product class is handled gracefully without interruption. Lastly, we check the errors list to see if it contains any messages. If it does, we convert all messages to a single string using String.Join() and send it to the log method. The error message that will be logged is: "Could not find member 'UPC' on object of type 'Product'. Path 'UPC', line 8, position 26".

If you feel more comfortable using lambda expressions, you can pass one to the event handler since it is just an anonymous function anyway. The syntax for using a lambda expression, shown in figure 3-30, is only slightly different than using a delegate.

```
Figure 3-30

Error = (object o, ErrorEventArgs e) =>
{
    errors.Add(e.ErrorContext.Error.Message);
    e.ErrorContext.Handled = true;
}
```

Another way to handle errors, is to assign a method name to the Error EventHandler property. In figure 3-31, we set the Error property of the JsonSerializerSettings object to the method name of “HandleErrors”. Then, we defined the HandleErrors() method which does the same thing as the inline methods in the previous examples. Notice the method must have the correct signature for event handlers, accepting a sender object and an EventArgs object, in our case, Json.NET's ErrorEventArgs. When the code is run, the same error message is sent to the logging method.

```
Figure 3-31

public void Go()
{
    var jStr = @"{
            ""Name"": ""Shirt"",
            ""Stock"": ""5"",
            ""Sizes"": [
                ""Large"",
                ""Medium""
            ],
            ""UPC"": ""123456789""
        }";

    var settings = new JsonSerializerSettings
    {
        MissingMemberHandling = MissingMemberHandling.Error,
        Error = HandleErrors
    };

    var prod =
            JsonConvert.DeserializeObject<Product>(jStr, settings);
}

private void HandleErrors(object sender, ErrorEventArgs errorArgs)
{
    log(errorArgs.ErrorContext.Error.Message);
    //mark error as handled or exception is thrown
    errorArgs.ErrorContext.Handled = true;
}
```

ConstructorHandling

The ConstructorHandling setting allows a class to use a private constructor when deserializing. A class with only private constructors and no public constructors cannot be instantiated. Private constructors are more useful when using patterns or with a class containing only static members. We cooked-up an admittedly contrived example using private constructors in order to keep the code simple demonstrating use of the ConstructorHandling setting.

The Product class in figure 3-32 has both a private constructor and a public constructor. The private constructor initializes the Stock and Sizes properties, while the public constructor sets the Name property with a parameter.

```
Figure 3-32

public class Product
{
    public string Name { get; set; }
    public int Stock { get; set; }
    public List<string> Sizes { get; set; }

    private Product()
    {
        Stock = 5;
        Sizes = new List<string>() { "Small", "Medium" };
    }

    public Product(string name)
    {
        Name = name;
    }
}
```

Let's see what happens when Json.NET deserializes JSON using the public constructor by default. The source JSON in figure 3-33 contains only a Name item.

```
Figure 3-33

public void Go()
{
    var jsonStr = @"{
        ""Name"": ""Shirt"",
    }";

    var prodObj = JsonConvert.DeserializeObject<Product>(jsonStr);
}
```

When this JSON is deserialized, the prodObj would result in figure 3-34. Since the public constructor is used by default, only the Name property received a value. Both the Sizes and Stock properties contain their default values.

```
Figure 3-34

prodObj:
    Name        = "Shirt"
    Sizes       = null
    Stock       = 0
```

Let's instruct Json.NET to deserialize using the private constructor by creating a JsonSerializerSettings object and setting the ConstructorHandling property to enum AllowNonPublicDefaultConstructor, as shown in figure 3-35.

```
Figure 3-35

public void Go()
{
    var jsonStr = @"{
        ""Name"": ""Shirt"",
    }";

    var settings = new JsonSerializerSettings
    {
        ConstructorHandling =
                 ConstructorHandling.AllowNonPublicDefaultConstructor
    };

    var prodObj =
            JsonConvert.DeserializeObject<Product>(jsonStr, settings);
}
```

This time, Json.NET will use the private constructor when deserializing, which initializes the Stock and Sizes property. This time, prodObj would result in figure 3-36, with all three properties containing the proper values.

```
Figure 3-36

prodObj:
    Name        = "Shirt"
    Sizes       = Count = 2
    Stock       = 5
```

{

"Chapter" : "Four",

"Title" : "Json Attributes"

}

Json.NET allows you to control the serialization/deserialization process through the use of attributes to decorate your .NET class or property declarations. Keep in mind when using attributes, C# lets you omit the "Attribute" suffix, as well as empty constructor parenthesis. So the attribute decorations in figure 4-1 all accomplish the same thing:

```
Figure 4-1

[Serializable]
public String Name { get; set; }

[Serializable()]
public String Name { get; set; }

[SerializableAttribute]
public String Name { get; set; }

[SerializableAttribute()]
public String Name { get; set; }
```

JsonProperty

JsonProperty is an attribute used to decorate class properties to control serialization. The JsonPropertyAttribute class contains many different properties that you can set by passing them as attribute constructor arguments. To use them is quite simple, just define the JsonProperty attribute above the property definition, as shown in figure 4-2.

```
Figure 4-2

public class Product
{
    [JsonProperty(Required=Required.Always)]
    public String Name { get; set; }

    [JsonProperty(PropertyName="Name")]
    public String ProductName { get; set; }
```

Or, you can define multiple JsonProperties by separating them with a comma, as shown in figure 4-3.

```
Figure 4-3

public class Product
{
    [JsonProperty(Required=Required.Always, PropertyName="Name")]
    public String ProductName { get; set; }
```

JsonProperty(PropertyName)

To change a class property name in the JSON during serialization, use PropertyName, as shown in figure 4-4. Here, we want the Name property to become ProductName in the JSON. We add a JsonProperty attribute over the Name property.

```
Figure 4-4

public class Product
{
    [JsonProperty(PropertyName = "ProductName")]
    public String Name { get; set; }
    public List<String> Sizes { get; set; }
    public int Stock { get; set; }
}

public class Class1
{
    public void Go()
    {
        var prodObj = new Product()
        {
```

```
            Name = "Shirt",
            Sizes = new List<string>() { "Small" }
        };

        var jsonStr = JsonConvert.SerializeObject(prodObj);
    }
}
```

So now when we instantiate a Product and serialize it, the JSON will contain its new name:

{"ProductName":"Shirt","Sizes":["Small"],"Stock":0,}

You can also specify a new name using this simpler syntax:

[JsonProperty("ProductName")]

JsonProperty(Required)

The Required property attribute is an enum that contains four values: Default, AllowNull, Always, DisallowNull. "Default" means the property is not required to be in the JSON, same as not setting it at all. "AllowNull" means the property must be defined in the JSON but may contain a null value. "Always" means the property must be defined in the JSON but may not contain a null value "DisallowNull" means the property is not required but if it exists, it cannot contain a null value.

To ensure that our Product Name is always written to the JSON but cannot be null, we marked it as Required.Always as shown in figure 4-5.

```
Figure 4-5

public class Product
{
    [JsonProperty(Required = Required.Always)]
    public String Name { get; set; }
    public List<String> Sizes { get; set; }
    public int Stock { get; set; }
}

public class Class1
{
    public void Go()
    {
        var prodStr = "{\"Sizes\":[\"Small\"]}";

        var prodOb =
                    JsonConvert.DeserializeObject<Product>(prodStr);
    }
}
```

Notice the source JSON in the prodStr variable does not contain a Name element, which is required. When we call the DeserializeObject() method it will throw a JsonSerializationException with the message: “Required property 'Name' not found in JSON”.

If the source JSON is modified to include a Name element that contains a null value, as in figure 4-6, it would still throw a JsonSerializationException but with a different message: “Required property 'Name' expects a value but got null.”

```
Figure 4-6

public void Go()
{
    var prodStr = "{\"Name\":null,\"Sizes\":[\"Small\"]}";

    var prodOb = JsonConvert.DeserializeObject<Product>(prodStr);
}
```

If the Required attribute was changed to AllowNull, as in figure 4-7, then the code would deserialize the JSON successfully.

```
Figure 4-7

public class Product
{
    [JsonProperty(Required = Required.AllowNull)]
    public String Name { get; set; }
    public List<String> Sizes { get; set; }
    public int Stock { get; set; }
}
```

JsonProperty - SerializerSettings

Using JsonProperty, you can also apply many of the same settings we used with JsonSerializerSettings, but it will apply to a specific property instead of the entire object. For example, we apply DefaultValueHandling to the Name property in figure 4-8. You can also pass args for NullValueHandling, ObjectCreationHandling, ReferenceLoopHandling and TypeNameHandling.

```
Figure 4-8

public class Product
{
    [JsonProperty(DefaultValueHandling =
                                      DefaultValueHandling.Ignore)]
    public String Name { get; set; }
```

Json.NET has other helpful serialization attributes to decorate your .NET class or properties. Let's take a look at some of them

JsonConstructorAttribute

The JsonConstructorAttribute allows you to specify which constructor you want to use during deserialization. By default, Json.NET will use the constructor without any parameters. If your class has overloaded constructors, decorate the constructor you want Json.NET to use with the [JsonConstructor] attribute.

For example, if the product JSON contains a positive value for Stock level, we want to set a flag in our class to indicate the item is in stock. The [JsonConstructor] attribute can help us do that by routing the deserialization process to use an overloaded constructor that will test the value for a valid stock level.

We added a boolean property to our Product class called inStock, as shown in figure 4-9. We also added a default constructor (no parameters) that tests the stock level and sets the value for the inStock boolean accordingly. Let's test this out and see if it does what we want.

Figure 4-9

```
public class Product
{
    public String Name { get; set; }
    public List<String> Sizes { get; set; }
    public int Stock { get; set; }
    public bool inStock { get; set; }

    public Product()
    {
        //this code will not work
        if (this.Stock > 0)
            inStock = true;
    }
}
```

The Go() method in figure 4-10 hasn't changed. It creates a JSON string and then deserializes it. Notice we are setting stock to 5, and there is no property in the JSON for the inStock boolean.

```
Figure 4-10

public void Go()
{
    //sample source JSON
    var jsonStr = @"{
        ""Name"": ""Shirt"",
        ""Sizes"": [""Large"", ""X-Large""],
        ""Stock"": 5
    }";

    var prodObj = JsonConvert.DeserializeObject<Product>(jsonStr);
}
```

When we run this code, the contents of the prodObj appears in figure 4-11. Hey! The stock got set to five, so how come inStock is still false? The problem is because the constructor is called before the deserialization process can set the value for Stock. All properties were initialized with default values, so Stock was set to zero, Name and Sizes were set to null. Because Stock was zero, the constructor set inStock to false. After deserialization, the properties were updated to the values contained in the JSON, so Stock was set to "5", Name was set to "Shirt" and Sizes to its two values. But the JSON did not contain an inStock property, so its value was left with false.

```
Figure 4-11

prodObj:
    inStock      = false
    Name         = "Shirt"
    Sizes        = Count = 2
    Stock        = 5
```

How do we fix this so it works like we want? We create an overloaded constructor and decorate it with the [JsonConstructor] attribute, as shown in figure 4-12, so it will be the one called during serialization.

```
Figure 4-12

public class Product
{
    public String Name { get; set; }
    public List<String> Sizes { get; set; }
    public int Stock { get; set; }
    public bool inStock { get; set; }

    public Product()
    {
    }
```

```
    [JsonConstructor]
    public Product(int stock)
    {
        this.Stock = stock;
        if (stock > 0)
            this.inStock = true;
    }
}
```

This time we run the Go() method and peek at the contents of prodObj, the inStock property is correctly set to true, as shown in figure 4-13.

```
Figure 4-13

prodObj:
    inStock      = true
    Name         = "Shirt"
    Sizes        = Count = 2
    Stock        = 5
```

So how come the overloaded constructor worked where the default constructor did not? Because when you use the [JsonConstructor] attribute, in addition to telling Json.NET which constructor to use, you can name the constructor parameter the same name as the JSON property. That way, Json.NET will automatically pass the value of the JSON property directly to the constructor!

Try it and see for yourself. Set a breakpoint on the beginning curly brace of both constructors and on the Go() method. Then start the debugger and step through the code in the Go() method. When you step to the line containing the DeserializeObject() method, the debugger steps-in to the overloaded constructor (notice the default constructor was skipped entirely). If you hover over the stock parameter, you will see it equals five. This is assigned to the Stock property and then it is tested to see if it is greater than zero. Since it is, the inStock property is set to true.

JsonObjectAttribute

The JsonObjectAttribute is used at the class level to control serialization. It can accept many different properties passed as arguments to its constructor. One of them is the MemberSerialization property. It is used to specify which properties are serialized to the JSON, even if they are marked private. MemberSerialization has three settings: OptIn, OptOut and Fields. "OptIn" means all properties decorated with [JsonProperty] will be included in the JSON. "OptOut" means properties decorated with [JsonIgnoreAttribute], or fields decorated with [NonSerialized], are NOT included in the JSON. "Fields" means all public and private fields will be serialized to the JSON.

JsonObject(MemberSerialization.OptIn)

Let's take a look at the OptIn process. We modified the Product class, as shown in Figure 4-14, by adding a class-level decoration for JsonObect, passing the MemberSerialization property set to OptIn as a constructor argument. We also added a private property for ID, which we initialize in the constructor. This means that only properties decorated with [JsonProperty] will be included in the JSON. In this case, we only decorated the Name property with the [JsonProperty] attribute.

Figure 4-14

```
[JsonObject(MemberSerialization = MemberSerialization.OptIn)]
public class Product
{
    private int Id { get; set; }
    [JsonProperty]
    public string Name { get; set; }
    public int Stock { get; set; }
    public List<string> Sizes { get; set; }

    public Product()
    {
        this.Id = 123;
    }
}

public class Class1
{
    public void Go()
    {
        var product = new Product()
        {
            Name = "Shirt",
            Sizes = new List<string>() { "Large", "Medium" },
            Stock = 5
        };
        var jsProd = JsonConvert.SerializeObject(product,
                        Formatting.Indented);
    }
}
```

In the Go() method, we create a product instance and serialize it. If we run this code, the JSON contents of the jsProd variable appears in figure 4-15. Since the

Name property was the only one decorated with the [JsonProperty] attribute, only Name was included in the JSON. Sizes, Stock and Id were excluded from the JSON.

```
Figure 4-15

{
  "Name": "Shirt"
}
```

Actually, the Id property was excluded because it was marked private. By default, private properties are not serialized to the JSON. To address this, let's add a [JsonProperty] attribute over the private Id property to "opt it back in", as shown in figure 4-16.

```
Figure 4-16

[JsonObject(MemberSerialization = MemberSerialization.OptIn)]
public class Product
{
    [JsonProperty]
    private int Id { get; set; }
    [JsonProperty]
    public string Name { get; set; }
    public int Stock { get; set; }
    public List<string> Sizes { get; set; }

    public Product()
    {
        this.Id = 123;
    }
}
```

This time, the private Id property is included in the JSON, as shown in figure 4-17.

```
Figure 4-17

{
  "Id": 123,
  "Name": "Shirt"
}
```

JsonObject(MemberSerialization.OptOut)

OptOut works a little bit differently in that you are marking properties to exclude them from the JSON. In figure 4-18, we changed the MemberSerialization enum to OptOut. Now all properties will be serialized to the JSON except for those decorated with an [JsonIgnore] attribute (*fields* can be decorated with [NonSerialized] attribute).

```
Figure 4-18

[JsonObject(MemberSerialization = MemberSerialization.OptOut)]
public class Product
{
    public string Name { get; set; }
    public int Stock { get; set; }
    [JsonIgnore]
    public List<string> Sizes { get; set; }
}

public class Class1
{
    public void Go()
    {
        var product = new Product()
        {
            Name = "Shirt",
            Sizes = new List<string>() { "Large", "Medium" },
            Stock = 5
        };
        var jsProd = JsonConvert.SerializeObject(product,
                         Formatting.Indented);
    }
}
```

Since only the Sizes property was decorated with a [JsonIgnore] attribute, Sizes does not appear in the JSON of figure 4-19. Name and Stock, which were not decorated, both appear in the JSON.

```
Figure 4-19

{
  "Name": "Shirt",
  "Stock": 5
}
```

JsonObject(MemberSerialization.Fields)

Setting MemberSerialization to Fields means all public and private fields will be serialized to the JSON. We altered the Product class to add some private and public fields, as well as getters/setters to encapsulate the private fields, as shown in figure 4-20.

```
Figure 4-20

public class Product
{
    private string _name;
    private int _stock;
    public string key;

    public string Name
    {
        get
        {
            return _name;
        }
        set
        {
            _name = value;
        }
    }

    public int Stock
    {
        get
        {
            return _stock;
        }
        set
        {
            _stock = value;
        }
    }
}

public class Class1
{
    public void Go()
    {
        var product = new Product()
        {
            Name = "Shirt",
            Stock = 5
        };
        var jsProd = JsonConvert.SerializeObject(product,
                        Formatting.Indented);
    }
}
```

If we serialized this class without a JsonObject MemberSerialization attribute set to Fields, the JSON it would produce appears in figure 4-21. As expected, the public Name and Stock properties were included in the JSON output. Notice the public key field was serialized, but not the two private fields.

```
Figure 4-21

{
  "key": null,
  "Name": "Shirt",
  "Stock": 5
}
```

Now let's alter the Product class again by setting MemberSerialization enum to Fields, as shown in figure 4-22.

```
Figure 4-22

[JsonObject(MemberSerialization = MemberSerialization.Fields)]
public class Product
{
    private string _name;
    private int _stock;
    public string key;

    public string Name
    {
        get
        {
            return _name;
        }
        set
        {
            _name = value;
        }
    }

    public int Stock
    {
        get
        {
            return _stock;
        }
        set
        {
            _stock = value;
        }
    }
}
```

Serializing the class would produce the JSON in figure 4-23. All three public and private fields were serialized to the JSON, but not the two public properties.

```
Figure 4-23
{
  "_name": "Shirt",
  "_stock": 5,
  "key": null
}
```

We can add the [JsonIgnore] attribute to any fields we want to exclude from the JSON. In figure 4-24, we added the attribute over the public key field and the private _stock field.

```
Figure 4-24

[JsonObject(MemberSerialization = MemberSerialization.Fields)]
public class Product
{
    private string _name;
    [JsonIgnore]
    private int _stock;
    [JsonIgnore]
    public string key;

    public string Name
    {
        get
        {
            return _name;
        }
        set
        {
            _name = value;
        }
    }

    public int Stock
    {
        get
        {
            return _stock;
        }
        set
        {
            _stock = value;
        }
    }
}
```

The JSON this would produce appears in figure 4-25. This time, only the _name private field was serialized to the JSON.

```
Figure 4-25

{
  "_name": "Shirt"
}
```

JsonObject IEnumerable

The JsonObject attribute can also be used on a class to force serialization to a JSON object, with curly braces {} on the root level. This is useful when the class implements the IEnumerable<T> interface. For the example, the code shown in figure 4-26, defines a simple Product class. We also define a new class called Products (plural) that implements IEnumerable<Product>. It has two properties, one for category name and one for a list of products in that particular category. The class also implements the interface's GetEnurmerator() method. The constructor of the Products class initializes the list of Products.

Our Go() method creates a Products object with a category of Apparel, and two products in the productsList. Then the products object is serialized to the prodJson variable.

```
Figure 4-26

public class Product
{
    public string Name { get; set; }
    public int Stock { get; set; }
    public List<string> Sizes { get; set; }
}

public class Products : IEnumerable<Product>
{
    public string Category { get; set; }
    public IList<Product> productsList { get; set; }

    public Products()
    {
        productsList = new List<Product>();
    }

    public IEnumerator<Product> GetEnumerator()
    {
        return productsList.GetEnumerator();
    }

    IEnumerator IEnumerable.GetEnumerator()
    {
        return GetEnumerator();
    }
}

public class Class1
{
    public void Go()
    {
        var products = new Products()
```

```
        {
            Category = "Apparel",
            productsList =
            {
                new Product()
                {
                    Name = "Shirt",
                    Sizes = new List<string>() { "Large", "Medium" },
                    Stock = 5
                },
                new Product()
                {
                    Name = "pants",
                    Sizes = new List<string>() { "33", "34" },
                    Stock = 9
                }
            }
        };
        var prodJson = JsonConvert.SerializeObject(products);
    }
}
```

If we were to run this code, the object would be serialized as a JSON array, with square brackets [] at the root level, as shown in figure 4-27. The Category property doesn't even appear in the JSON. It's as if the entire class was just serialized as a collection.

Figure 4-27

```
[
  {
    "Name": "Shirt",
    "Stock": 5,
    "Sizes": [
      "Large",
      "Medium"
    ]
  },
  {
    "Name": "pants",
    "Stock": 9,
    "Sizes": [
      "33",
      "34"
    ]
  }
]
```

But what if we wanted to serialize this as a JSON object, with curly braces {} at the root level? Then we would have to decorate the class with a [JsonObject] attribute, as shown in the first line of figure 4-28.

```
Figure 4-28

[JsonObject]
public class Products : IEnumerable<Product>
{
    public string Category { get; set; }
    public IList<Product> productsList { get; set; }

    public Products()
    {
        productsList = new List<Product>();
    }

    public IEnumerator<Product> GetEnumerator()
    {
        return productsList.GetEnumerator();
    }

    IEnumerator IEnumerable.GetEnumerator()
    {
        return GetEnumerator();
    }
}
```

This time when we run the code, the serialized JSON output would appear as in figure 4-29. This time, the output is a JSON object. There are now curly braces {} at the root level. Notice there is now a Category element, and the productsList element is still maintained as a JSON array.

```
Figure 4-29

{
  "Category": "Apparel",
  "productsList": [
    {
      "Name": "Shirt",
      "Stock": 5,
      "Sizes": [
        "Large",
        "Medium"
      ]
    },
    {
      "Name": "pants",
      "Stock": 9,
      "Sizes": [
        "33",
        "34"
      ]
    }
  ]
}
```

JsonObject(NamingStrategyType)

The JsonObject attribute also contains a NamingStrategyType property. It is used to specify the format (or Naming Strategy) of the serialized property names and/or dictionary key names. This attribute can decorate at the class level or the property level.

Json.NET includes three built-in implementations of the NamingStrategy abstract class: CamelCaseNamingStrategy which forces property names to begin with a lower case letter and capitalizes each new word, SnakeCaseNamingStrategy which uses lower case letters and separates words with an underscore, and the DefaultNamingStrategy where property names and dictionary keys are unchanged.

For this example, the Product class in figure 4-30 was decorated with the [JsonObject] attribute with NamingStrategyType property set to camel case. The property names were also modified to be longer and use Pascal casing.

```
Figure 4-30

[JsonObject(NamingStrategyType = typeof(CamelCaseNamingStrategy))]
public class Product
{
    public string ProductName { get; set; }
    public int StockLevel { get; set; }
    public List<string> SizesList { get; set; }
}
```

The code in figure 4-31 is the same serializing code we've seen before.

```
Figure 4-31

public void Go()
{
    var product = new Product()
    {
        ProductName = "Shirt",
        SizesList = new List<string>() { "Large", "Medium" },
        StockLevel = 5
    };
    var prodJson = JsonConvert.SerializeObject(product,
                   Formatting.Indented);
}
```

When we run the above code, the JSON contained in the prodJson variable is shown in figure 4-32. Notice all property names have been changed to camel casing. The first letter has been changed to lower case.

```
Figure 4-32

{
  "productName": "Shirt",
  "stockLevel": 5,
  "sizesList": [
    "Large",
    "Medium"
  ]
}
```

Now let's change the NamingStrategy to snake case, as shown in figure 4-33.

```
Figure 4-33

[JsonObject(NamingStrategyType = typeof(SnakeCaseNamingStrategy))]
public class Product
{
    public string ProductName { get; set; }
    public int StockLevel { get; set; }
    public List<string> SizesList { get; set; }
}
```

When we run the code again, the JSON contained in the prodJson variable appears in figure 4-34. Notice all property names have been changed to snake casing. All characters were changed to lower case and the words separated by an underscore.

```
Figure 4-34

{
  "product_name": "Shirt",
  "stock_level": 5,
  "sizes_list": [
    "Large",
    "Medium"
  ]
}
```

JsonExtensionDataAttribute - Deserialization

The JsonExtensionDataAttribute must decorate a dictionary property. Then, during deserialization, Json.NET will dump all the properties that are missing from the deserialization class into this collection.

Let's see how this would work. In figure 4-35, we added a dictionary property named missingMembers to our Product class and decorated it with the [JsonExtensionData] attribute. In our Go() method, we create a product JSON string with a couple extra properties, UPC and Price, that are not defined in our Product class. Next, the product JSON is deserialized to the Product class.

Because UPC and Price are not defined in the class, using the JsonExtensionData attribute will automatically add both UPC and Price to the missingMembers dictionary.

```
Figure 4-35

public class Product
{
    public string Name { get; set; }
    public int Stock { get; set; }
    public List<string> Sizes { get; set; }

    [JsonExtensionData]
    public Dictionary<string, JToken> missingMembers;
}

public class Class1
{
    public void Go()
    {
        var jsonStr = @"{
            ""Name"": ""Shirt"",
            ""Stock"": ""5"",
            ""Sizes"": [
                ""Large"",
                ""Medium""
            ],
            ""UPC"": ""123456789"",
            ""Price"": 19.99
        }";
        var prodObj =
                    JsonConvert.DeserializeObject<Product>(jsonStr);
        var output = String.Join(" | ", prodObj.missingMembers
            .Select(d => d.Key + " : " + d.Value).ToArray());
    }
}
```

Then, Linq is used to grab all the items from the dictionary and format them into a readable string. When this code is run, the output variable will contain the string: "UPC : 123456789 | Price : 19.99".

JsonExtensionDataAttribute - Serialization

During serialization, using the [JsonExtensionData] attribute will ensure the key/value pairs in the dictionary are written back to the JSON object. Using the same Product class from Figure 4-35, we will just modify our Go() method to create a product instance, as shown in figure 4-36. Notice we initialize the missingMembers dictionary with two key/value pairs for UPC and Price (we discuss JToken Parse in a later chapter). Then we serialize the product object to a JSON string.

```
Figure 4-36

public void Go()
{
    var product = new Product()
    {
        Name = "Shirt",
        Sizes = new List<string>() { "Large", "Medium" },
        Stock = 5,
        missingMembers = new Dictionary<string, JToken>()
        {
            { "UPC", JToken.Parse("123456789").ToString()},
            { "Price", JToken.Parse("19.99")}
        }
    };
    var prodJson = JsonConvert.SerializeObject(product,
                        Formatting.Indented);
}
```

The contents of the prodJson variable appear in figure 4-37. Notice UPC and Price properties were written to the JSON as normal key/value pairs, just like our original jsonStr source back in figure 4-35.

```
Figure 4-37

{
  "Name": "Shirt",
  "Stock": 5,
  "Sizes": [
    "Large",
    "Medium"
  ],
  "UPC": "123456789",
  "Price": 19.99
}
```

JsonConverterAttribute

The JsonConverterAttribute can be used on both classes and properties to instruct Json.NET to invoke a specific JsonConverter. We go into more details on JsonConverters in the next chapter, but basically they let you customize the serialization process. Json.NET comes with a lot of useful pre-built converters that can be applied to a class or property. Json.NET also allows you to build your own custom JsonConverters. For demonstration purposes, we use the attribute to invoke the pre-built StringEnumConverter. This converter is used to print the string equivalent of an enum.

In figure 4-38, we declare an enum named Status that has three values. We then add a new ProdStatus property to our Product class using the new enum. Our Go() method just instantiates a product object and serializes it.

```
Figure 4-38

public enum Status
{
    Pre_Order,
    Out_Of_Stock,
    In_Stock
};

public class Product
{
    public string Name { get; set; }
    public int Stock { get; set; }
    public List<string> Sizes { get; set; }
    public Status ProdStatus { get; set; }

}

public class Class1
{
    public void Go()
    {
        var prodObj = new Product()
        {
            Name = "Shirt",
            Stock = 5,
            Sizes = new List<string>() { "Small" },
            ProdStatus = Status.In_Stock
        };

        var jsonStr = JsonConvert.SerializeObject(prodObj,
                               Formatting.Indented);
    }
}
```

If we were to run this code as-is, without using a JsonConverter attribute, the JSON would appear as in figure 4-39. Notice the value for ProdStatus is "2". Not very helpful. It would not be long before we forgot what "2" represents. It would be more beneficial if the value contained the enum string equivalent.

```
Figure 4-39

{
  "Name": "Shirt",
  "Stock": 5,
  "Sizes": [
```

```
    "Small"
  ],
  "ProdStatus": 2
}
```

Let's modify the Product class by adding a JsonConverter attribute over the ProdStatus property, as shown in figure 4-40. Notice we pass the StringEnumConverter type in the parenthesis of the JsonConverter attribute constructor.

Be sure to add a using directive for: using Newtonsoft.Json.Converters;

```
Figure 4-40

public class Product
{
    public string Name { get; set; }
    public int Stock { get; set; }
    public List<string> Sizes { get; set; }
    [JsonConverter(typeof(StringEnumConverter))]
    public Status ProdStatus { get; set; }

}
```

This time when we run the Go() method, the JSON in figure 4-41 confirms that invoking the StringEnumConverter has written the value of the ProdStatus enum using its more readable string equivalent.

```
Figure 4-41

{
  "Name": "Shirt",
  "Stock": 5,
  "Sizes": [
    "Small"
  ],
  "ProdStatus": "In_Stock"
}
```

{

"Chapter" : "Five",

"Title" : "JsonConverter class"

}

JsonConverters extend or customize the serialization/deserialization process. Json.NET comes with several pre-built converters, or you can build your own custom converter by deriving from the JsonConverter abstract class. There are three abstract methods you must implement: ReadJson(), WriteJson() and CanConvert(). The WriteJson() method is called during serialization. The ReadJson() method is called during deserialization. The CanConvert() method is called to see if the converter can process the specified object type. The bare minimum implementation appears in figure 5-1, though it is not very useful as it stands.

```
Figure 5-1

public class MyConverter : JsonConverter
{
    public override bool CanConvert(Type objectType)
    {
        return false;
```

```
    }

    public override void WriteJson(JsonWriter writer,
        object value, JsonSerializer serializer)
    {
        throw new NotImplementedException();
    }

    public override object ReadJson(JsonReader reader,
        Type objectType, object existingValue,
        JsonSerializer serializer)
    {
        return null;
    }
}
```

To invoke the JsonConverter for a single property is very simple. Just add an attribute to the class property, along with the converter name, as shown in figure 5-2.

```
Figure 5-2

[JsonConverter(typeof(MyConverter))]
public List<String> Sizes { get; set; }
```

One of the helpful uses of JsonConverters is to fix bad data in third-party JSON. A common scenario involves JSON arrays. For example, third-party JSON from an API may contain a properties that hold an array of objects. Consequently, you would define the corresponding property in your serialization class to hold an array. After a few days, you notice your code randomly throws an error. After debugging, you discover it is because there are times when the third-party JSON returns a single JSON object *instead* of an *array* with 1 item. Naturally, our class is expecting an array to convert to a collection, not an object, so it throws an exception during deserialization.

Even if you submit a bug ticket to the third-party about the JSON issue in their API (politely not mentioning the hours you wasted tracking down their bug), it may be very low on their priority list to fix. However, it remains a huge problem for your application. Sometimes it is easier and faster to apply a fix on your end using a custom JsonConverter to convert any single objects back into a collection. The code for our custom JsonConverter class appears in figure 5-3.

```
Figure 5-3

public class MyConverter : JsonConverter
{
    public override bool CanWrite { get { return false; } }
```

```
    //not called when invoked by attribute
    public override bool CanConvert(Type objectType)
    {
        return (objectType == typeof(MyConverter));
    }

    public override void WriteJson(JsonWriter writer,
        object value, JsonSerializer serializer)
    {
        throw new NotImplementedException();
    }

    public override object ReadJson(JsonReader reader,
        Type objectType, object existingValue,
        JsonSerializer serializer)
    {
        if (reader.TokenType == JsonToken.StartArray)
        {
            //all good, send back what came
            return serializer.Deserialize(reader, objectType);
        }
        else
        {
            var jObj = JObject.Load(reader);
            //if unexpected results, just send back what came
            if (jObj == null || jObj.Count == 0 || !jObj.HasValues)
                return serializer.Deserialize(reader, objectType);

            //we know the object can be deserialized to Product class
            var product = jObj.ToObject<Product>();
            return new List<Product>() { product };
        }
    }
}
```

When you invoke a JsonConverter via attribute, as we are doing in this example, the CanConvert() method is not called to check if the object is convertible, because Json.NET assumes you are calling the correct converter for the object. If we were to embed multiple converters in a JsonSerializerSettings object, as discussed in the previous chapter, then the CanConvert() would be called to check every property in the class. Since the method must be implemented, regardless, it doesn't hurt to add the appropriate logic, just in case the converter is re-used in a JsonSerializerSettings object.

Our first example focuses on serialization. Therefore, the WriteJson() method of the custom converter in figure 5-3 will not be called and was left empty. To make doubly sure the WriteJson() method is not called, we implemented the CanWrite property and overrode it to always return false. Alternatively, it is not a bad idea to implement the WriteJson() method to just return whatever was passed into the method. The code to do that appears in figure 5-4, but make sure you delete the CanWrite override from your class. And don't forget to add a using directive to use the JToken class: using Newtonsoft.Json.Linq;

```
Figure 5-4

public override void WriteJson(JsonWriter writer, object value,
     JsonSerializer serializer)
{
    //do normal serialization
    var token = JToken.FromObject(value);
    token.WriteTo(writer);
}
```

The ReadJson() method in figure 5-3 is where all the action occurs during serialization. The first thing it does is check to see if the element is a JSON array. If it is, we simply return the same data that was passed in. If it is not a JSON array, we need to place the object in a new collection and return it. This will ensure our application successfully deserializes both scenarios: when the source JSON object contains an array, or whether it contains a single object.

Let's take a look at the code that will make use of this custom JsonConverter. In figure 5-5, we create a new ProductsList class with a single property to hold a list of Products. Notice we've decorated the property with a JsonConverter attribute with the type for our converter class. This will invoke our custom converter only on the Products property.

```
Figure 5-5

public class ProductsList
{
    [JsonConverter(typeof(MyConverter))]
    public List<Product> Products { get; set; }
}
```

The application code appears in figure 5-6 with a couple of new private methods. The main Go() method pretty much remains the same. It just fetches JSON and deserializes it to a C# class. Remember, the main work will be done in the MyConverter class we created.

```
Figure 5-6

public class Class1
{
    public void Go()
    {
```

```
        //simulate JSON source
        var jsonStr = SimulateProductsArrayJson();

        var newObj =
            JsonConvert.DeserializeObject<ProductsList>(jsonStr);
    }

    private string SimulateProductsArrayJson()
    {
        //simulate JSON for array of 2 products
        return @"
        {
            ""Products"":
            [
                {
                    ""Name"": ""Shirt"",
                    ""Sizes"": [""Medium"", ""Large""]
                },
                {
                    ""Name"": ""Pants"",
                    ""Sizes"": [""31"", ""33""]
                }
            ]
        }";
    }

    private string SimulateProductObjectJson()
    {
        //simulate JSON for 1 product
        return @"
        {
            ""Products"":
                {
                    ""Name"": ""Shirt"",
                    ""Sizes"": [""Medium"", ""Large""]
                }
        }";
    }
}
```

The two new helper methods just return JSON that we'd expect to get from a third-party API. The first method SimulateProductsArrayJson() returns JSON where the Products property is a JSON array containing two products. The second method SimulateProductObjectJson() returns JSON where the Products property is a simple object containing one product. The two JSON examples appear in figure 5-7.

```
Figure 5-7

//Products as an array
{
  "Products": [
    {
      "Name": "Shirt",
      "Sizes": [
        "Medium",
```

```
        "Large"
      ]
    },
    {
      "Name": "Pants",
      "Sizes": [
        "31",
        "33"
      ]
    }
  ]
}

//Products as an object
{
  "Products": {
    "Name": "Shirt",
    "Sizes": [
      "Medium",
      "Large"
    ]
  }
}
```

Now keep in mind, even if we didn't use the JsonConverter, the JSON from the SimulateProductsArrayJson() method would deserialize just fine, because the deserialization class ProductsList in figure 5-5 is expecting a JSON array to convert into a List<T>. This is the normal "happy path". If we ran the code in figure 5-6 that deserializes a Products array, it would execute successfully. If we were to peek at the data contents of the resulting object, it would appear as in figure 5-8.

```
Figure 5-8

newObj:
     Products:
     [0]:
               Name        = "Shirt"
               Sizes       = Count 2
               Stock       = 0
     [1]:
               Name        = "Pants"
               Sizes       = Count 2
               Stock       = 0
```

The problem comes when we change the source JSON method to SimulateProductObjectJson(). This method returns JSON with a single Product object instead of an array. This will cause a JsonSerializationException because an object does not deserialize into a C# collection. Let's run code that we know will break. Comment out the JsonConvert attribute in the ProductsList class and change the method name as shown in figure 5-9. If you run the code now, it will throw an exception because the deserializer is expecting a JSON array to convert to a List<T>, but all it gets is a single JSON product object.

```
Figure 5-9

public void Go()
{
    //simulate JSON source
    var jsonStr = SimulateProductObjectJson();

    var newObj =
            JsonConvert.DeserializeObject<ProductsList>(jsonStr);
}
```

Now uncomment the JsonConvert attribute to "enable" our custom JsonConverter and run the code again. This time, the JsonConverter ReadJson() method detects the single product object and converts it to a single-item collection so deserialization is successful. If we were to peek at the data contents of the resulting object, it would appear as in figure 5-10.

```
Figure 5-10

newObj:
    Products:
    [0]:
            Name        = "Shirt"
            Sizes       = Count 2
            Stock       = 0
```

Now your application is "third-party proof" and can handle both types of JSON scenarios returned from the API. And you didn't even have to contact their tech support team!

Json.NET comes with some handy pre-built JsonConverters in the Newtonsoft.Json.Converters namespace. These all inherit from the JsonConverter abstract class, which is in the main Newtonsoft.Json namespace. A couple pre-built JsonConverters of interest are the JavaScriptDateTimeConverter class and the IsoDateTimeConverter class. (Technically, these DateTime converters inherit from the DateTimeConverterBase abstract class, which in turn inherits the JsonConverter abstract class).

Both the SerializeObject() method and the DeserializeObject() method have an overload that accepts an array of JsonConverters. So you can pass there pre-built converters directly to the serialize/deserialize methods. Let's take a look at how to use these handy built-in converters.

JavaScriptDateTimeConverter

The products class in figure 5-11 has been modified by adding three new DateTime properties.

```
Figure 5-11

public class Product
{
    public String Name { get; set; }
    public List<String> Sizes { get; set; }
    public int Stock { get; set; }
    public DateTime CreateDate { get; set; }
    public DateTime ModifyDate { get; set; }
    public DateTime RetireDate { get; set; }
}
```

The new DateTime properties are initialized with different dates, as shown in Figure 5-12.

```
Figure 5-12

class Class1
{
    public void Go()
    {
        var prodObj = new Product()
        {
            Name = "Shirt",
            Stock = 5,
            Sizes = new List<string>() { "Small" },
            CreateDate = new DateTime(2012, 1, 18, 17, 22, 35,
                                DateTimeKind.Utc),
            RetireDate = new DateTime(2015, 12, 21, 11, 59, 59,
                                DateTimeKind.Utc),
            ModifyDate = new DateTime(2013, 7, 22, 9, 43, 12,
                                DateTimeKind.Utc)
        };

        var jsonStr = JsonConvert.SerializeObject(prodObj);
    }
}
```

If we ran the code above *without* using a JavaScriptDateTimeConverter in the SerializeObject() method, the JSON contained in the the jsonStr variable would appear as shown in Figure 5-13. The date values all appear in ISO 8601 format, since that is the default format.

```
Figure 5-13 - ISO 8601 Date Format

{
  "Name": "Shirt",
  "Sizes": [
    "Small"
  ],
  "Stock": 5,
  "CreateDate": "2012-01-18T17:22:35Z",
  "ModifyDate": "2013-07-22T09:43:12Z",
  "RetireDate": "2015-12-21T11:59:59Z"
}
```

If we were to pass a JavaScriptDateTimeConverter to the SerializeObject() method, as shown in the last line of figure 5-14, the date values in the resulting JSON would then be JavaScript date objects, as shown in figure 5-15.

```
Figure 5-14

public void Go()
{
    var prodObj = new Product()
    {
        Name = "Shirt",
        Stock = 5,
        Sizes = new List<string>() { "Small" },
        CreateDate = new DateTime(2012, 1, 18, 17, 22, 35,
                          DateTimeKind.Utc),
        RetireDate = new DateTime(2015, 12, 21, 11, 59, 59,
                          DateTimeKind.Utc),
        ModifyDate = new DateTime(2013, 7, 22, 9, 43, 12,
                          DateTimeKind.Utc)
    };

    var jsonStr = JsonConvert.SerializeObject(prodObj,
            new JavaScriptDateTimeConverter());
}
```

```
Figure 5-15 - JavaScript Date Objects

{
  "Name": "Shirt",
  "Sizes": [
    "Small"
  ],
  "Stock": 5,
  "CreateDate": newDate(1326936155000),
  "ModifyDate": newDate(1374511392000),
  "RetireDate": newDate(1450727999000)
}
```

IsoDateTimeConverter

If we were to pass a IsoDateTimeConverter to the SerializeObject() method, as shown in the last line of figure 5-16, the date values in the resulting JSON would be the same as figure 5-13, since ISO 8601 is the default date format. The ISO 8601 standard became the default Json.NET date format starting with Json.NET 4.5. Prior to that, the IsoDateTimeConverter was a little more useful because the default date format of Json.NET was the Microsoft Date format: "\/Date(1234656000000)\/".

```
Figure 5-16

public void Go()
{
    var prodObj = new Product()
    {
        Name = "Shirt",
        Stock = 5,
        Sizes = new List<string>() { "Small" },
        CreateDate = new DateTime(2012, 1, 18, 17, 22, 35,
                              DateTimeKind.Utc),
        RetireDate = new DateTime(2015, 12, 21, 11, 59, 59,
                              DateTimeKind.Utc),
        ModifyDate = new DateTime(2013, 7, 22, 9, 43, 12,
                              DateTimeKind.Utc)
    };

    var jsonStr = JsonConvert.SerializeObject(prodObj,
            new IsoDateTimeConverter());
}
```

StringEnumConverter

StringEnumConverter is useful when you want to display the text of the enum instead of the integer value. To demonstrate this, we've added another property to the Product class, an enum for ProductStatus, as shown in figure 5-17.

```
Figure 5-17

public enum Status
{
    Pre_Order,
    Out_Of_Stock,
    In_Stock
};

public class Product
{
    public String Name { get; set; }
```

```
    public List<String> Sizes { get; set; }
    public int Stock { get; set; }
    public Status ProdStatus { get; set; }
}
```

The application code in figure 5-18 makes use of the new status enum.

```
Figure 5-18

class Class1
{
    public void Go()
    {
        var prodObj = new Product()
        {
            Name = "Shirt",
            Stock = 5,
            Sizes = new List<string>() { "Small" },
            ProdStatus = Status.In_Stock
        };

        var jsonStr = JsonConvert.SerializeObject(prodObj);
    }
}
```

Now if we were to run the code in figure 5-18 without passing the StringEnumConverter to the SerializeObject() method, the JSON would contain a number for ProdStatus, as shown in figure 5-19.

```
Figure 5-19

{
  "Name": "Shirt",
  "Sizes": [
    "Small"
  ],
  "Stock": 5,
  "ProdStatus": 2
}
```

Well, that isn't very intuitive. We would soon forget what a "2" represents. We would like the JSON to instead contain the string value of the enum. Let's alter the SerializeObject() method and pass it the StringEnumConverter, as shown in the last line of figure 5-20.

```
Figure 5-20

class Class1
{
    public void Go()
    {
        var prodObj = new Product()
        {
            Name = "Shirt",
            Stock = 5,
            Sizes = new List<string>() { "Small" },
```

```
            ProdStatus = Status.In_Stock
        };

        var jsonStr = JsonConvert.SerializeObject(prodObj,
                new StringEnumConverter());
    }
}
```

Now when we run this code, the JSON in the jsonStr variable, shown in figure 5-21, contains the string value of the enum in the ProdStatus property.

```
Figure 5-21

{
  "Name": "Shirt",
  "Sizes": [
    "Small"
  ],
  "Stock": 5,
  "ProdStatus": "In_Stock"
}
```

DataSetConverter and DataTableConverter

Both DataSetConverter and DataTableConverter are used internally whenever you serialize or deserialize a DataSet. This is illustrated in figure 5-22. The GetDataSet() method returns a mocked-up product DataSet, which is then passed to the SerializeObject() method. Json.NET would internally call the DataSetConverter and DataTableConverter when serializing the data.

```
Figure 5-22

public void Go()
{
    var ds = GetDataSet();

    //uses DataSetConverter internally
    var dsObj = JsonConvert.SerializeObject(ds);
}

public DataSet GetDataSet()
{
    var table1 = new DataTable("products");
    table1.Columns.Add("id");
    table1.Columns.Add("name");
    table1.Rows.Add(1, "Shirt");
    table1.Rows.Add(2, "Pants");

    var table2 = new DataTable("sizes");
```

```
    table2.Columns.Add("id");
    table2.Columns.Add("productId");
    table2.Columns.Add("sizeName");
    table2.Rows.Add(1, 1, "Large");
    table2.Rows.Add(2, 1, "Small");
    table2.Rows.Add(3, 2, "33");

    // Create a DataSet and put both tables in it.
    var ds = new DataSet();
    ds.Tables.Add(table1);
    ds.Tables.Add(table2);
    return ds;
}
```

The JSON it produces is displayed in figure 5-23. Notice the two distinct DataTables are serialized as two separate JSON arrays.

Figure 5-23

```
{
  "products": [
    {
      "id": "1",
      "name": "Shirt"
    },
    {
      "id": "2",
      "name": "Pants"
    }
  ],
  "sizes": [
    {
      "id": "1",
      "productId": "1",
      "sizeName": "Large"
    },
    {
      "id": "2",
      "productId": "1",
      "sizeName": "Small"
    },
    {
      "id": "3",
      "productId": "2",
      "sizeName": "33"
    }
  ]
}
```

Keep in mind, you can have also invoke JsonConverters by using a property attribute decoration, as shown in figure 5-24. In fact, anytime you invoke a JsonConverter via an attribute, it is faster than passing it as a method parameter.

When a JsonConverter is passed as a method parameter, the CanConvert() method must be called for every value.

```
Figure 5-24

public class Product
{
    public String Name { get; set; }
    public List<String> Sizes { get; set; }
    public int Stock { get; set; }
    [JsonConverter(typeof(StringEnumConverter))]
    public Status ProdStatus { get; set; }
}
```

I hope this gives you an understanding of how to use some of the pre-built JsonConverters included with Json.NET, either invoked by property attribute or passed as a method parameter. The other pre-built JsonConverters all follow the same basic paradigm.

```
{
    "Chapter" : "Six",
    "Title" : [
                "JsonTextReader",
                "JsonTextWriter"
              ]
}
```

The hands-down quickest way to read and write JSON is to use the JsonTextReader/JsonTextWriter classes directly. This is because, unlike JsonConvert and JsonSerializer, JsonTextReader/JsonTextWriter does not use Reflection.

JsonTextWriter

If you are at all concerned with performance, then instead of calling the JsonConvert.SerializeObject() method to produce JSON, you can manually build the JSON using JsonTextWriter. But we aware, this requires many more lines of code and can become quite tedious for complex JSON.

Let's start by writing some JSON based on the Product class, as depicted in figure 6-1. Don't forget to add a using directive to use the StringWriter:

using System.IO;

```
Figure 6-1

class Class1
{
    public void Go()
    {
        var prodObj = new Product()
        {
            Name = "Shirt",
            Sizes = new List<string>() { "Small", "Medium" },
            Stock = 5
        };

        var jsonStr = WriteJson(prodObj);
    }

    public string WriteJson(Product product)
    {
        var sb = new StringBuilder();
        var sw = new StringWriter(sb);
        using (var writer = new JsonTextWriter(sw))
        {
            writer.Formatting = Formatting.Indented;
            writer.WriteStartObject();

            // "Name"
            writer.WritePropertyName("Name");
            writer.WriteValue(product.Name);

            // "Stock"
            writer.WritePropertyName("Stock");
            writer.WriteValue(product.Stock);

            // "Sizes"
            writer.WritePropertyName("Sizes");
            writer.WriteStartArray();
            foreach (string size in product.Sizes)
            {
                writer.WriteValue(size);
            }
            writer.WriteEndArray();

            writer.WriteEndObject();
        }
        return sb.ToString();
    }
}
```

Notice that the Go() method looks pretty much like it has in the past. It simply creates a product instance and then serializes it. But this time, instead of calling

JsonConvert.SerializeObject(), we wrote our our serialization method called WriteJson().

The WriteJson() method starts by creating objects for StringBuilder and StringWriter and passing it to JsonTextWriter. We set the Formatting property to Indented so our JSON will be nicely formatted. The Formatting needs to be done before writing starts. Formatting will not be honored if defined after writing has completed.

First, the WriteStartObject() method is called. This produces the beginning curly brace that denotes a JSON object. Notice at the very end of the code block, we call its companion WriteEndObject() method, which produces the closing curly brace.

Next, two methods are called to create a JSON element: WritePropertyName() and WriteValue(). The Name and Stock elements are created accordingly. Since the Sizes property is a list with multiple values, we must create an array object by calling WriteStartArray(), which produces the starting square bracket of an array, and then close the array by calling WriteEndArray(), which produces the closing square bracket. In between, we loop through the Sizes collection and call WriteValue() for each item.

When we run this code, the JSON it produces appears in figure 6-2.

```
Figure 6-2

{
  "Name": "Shirt",
  "Stock": 5,
  "Sizes": [
    "Small",
    "Medium"
  ]
}
```

The cool thing about JsonTextWriter is that it will warn you if you try to write invalid JSON. For example, comment out the line where the WriteEndArray() method is called and run the program again. This time a JsonWriterException is thrown with the message "Token PropertyName in state Array would result in an invalid JSON object". It is nice to know that JsonTextWriter has your back!

JsonTextReader

The quickest way to read JSON, such as when deserializing, is to use the JsonTextReader directly. So let's take the JSON we just created and manually deserialize it back to the Product class as shown in the code in the figure 6-3.

```
Figure 6-3

class Class1
{
    public void Go()
    {
        //sample source JSON
        var jsonStr = @"{
            ""Name"": ""Shirt"",
            ""Sizes"": [
            ""Small"",
            ""Medium""
            ],
            ""Stock"": 5
        }";

        var newObj = ReadJson(jsonStr);
    }

    public Product ReadJson(string jsonStr)
    {
        var prod = new Product(){Sizes = new List<string>()};
        var reader = new JsonTextReader(new StringReader(jsonStr));
        while (reader.Read())
        {
            if (reader.Value != null)
            {
                if (reader.TokenType == JsonToken.PropertyName
                        && reader.Value.ToString() == "Name")
                {
                    reader.Read();
                    prod.Name = reader.Value.ToString();
                }
                else if (reader.TokenType == JsonToken.PropertyName
                        && reader.Value.ToString() == "Stock")
                {
                    reader.Read();
                    prod.Stock =
                        Convert.ToInt32(reader.Value.ToString());
                }
                else if (reader.TokenType == JsonToken.PropertyName
                        && reader.Value.ToString() == "Sizes")
                {
                    do
                    {
                        reader.Read();
                        if (reader.Value != null)
                            prod.Sizes.Add(reader.Value.ToString());
                    } while (reader.TokenType != JsonToken.EndArray);
                }
```

```
            }
        }
        return prod;
    }
```

In the Go() method, the product JSON is sent to the ReadJson() method, which will return a Product object.

The ReadJson() method starts out by instantiating a product instance and initializing the Size collection. Since the JsonTextReader constructor only accepts a TextReader and not a JSON string, we must first pass the JSON string to the StringReader constructor, because StringReader derives from TextReader.

Then we loop through the reader, for every item in the JSON. We first check if the reader.Value is null. If reader.Value is null, it can represent either the opening or closing curly brace, and reader.TokenType would then be equal to StartObject or EndObject. But that is not something we need concern ourselves for deserializing the Product class, so we can ignore it when reader.Value is null.

When reader.Value is not null, then we want to check the reader.TokenType. If it contains "PropertyName", we then check reader.Value to see which element we are dealing with. If reader.Value is equal to "Name", then we know we need to populate the Product.name property. To get the value for the "Name" element, we need to look at the next iteration of the reader, so we call reader.Read() to advance to the next item. Behind the scenes, the new reader.TokenType will be "String", which is the type we expect. Now we can set Product.Name to the contents of reader.Value.

A similar approach is taken with the "Stock" element. We check for a TokenType of PropertyName and value equal to "Stock". The we iterate to get the next item in the reader. The TokenType will now be "Integer". We assign Product.Stock with the contents of reader.Value.

The approach for Sizes is a little more involved since it involves processing an array. After we confirm TokenType and value, we enter a do/while loop which will loop until the TokenType is EndArray, signaling, of course, an end to the array elements.

The first thing the loop does is get the next item by calling reader.Read(). This item will be the square bracket "[" signaling the start of an array. The TokenType will be "StartArray" and its reader.Value will be null. So we can skip this item by testing for not null. The loop will continue and make another call to reader.Read() to get the next item. The next item will be a TokenType of String whose value we will add to our list of sizes.

The loop is repeated until reader.Value turns up null again. Then we know it is an EndArray TokenType which will cause our loop to end. The populated Product object is then returned to the caller.

This ReadJson() method implementation places a hard dependency on the Products class, so it is probably not something you'd want to use in production. It does, however, keep the code example simple to demonstrate the point.

{

"Chapter" : "Seven",

"Title" : "JsonSerializer Class"

}

For advanced control over serializing an object or deserializing to string, you want to use the JsonSerializer class directly. In fact, the methods in the JsonConvert class ultimately end up wrapping JsonSerializer functionality.

JsonSerializer reads JSON from a stream using derived objects from the JsonReader abstract class, such as the JsonTextReader, BsonReader or JTokenReader classes. The serialize methods of JsonSerializer all accept an object to serialize, as well as a stream to write to, in the form of JsonWriter object or a System.IO.TextWriter object.

JsonSerializer writes JSON to a stream using derived objects from the JsonWriter abstract class, such as the JsonTextWriter, BsonWriter or JTokenWriter classes. When deserializing with JsonSerializer, it is important to remember that it does not accept a JSON string, it accepts only a JsonReader object or a System.IO.TextReader object.

Also, unlike the SerializeObject() and DeserializeObject() methods of the JsonConvert class, there is no need to create and pass a JsonSerializerSettings object. The same JsonSerializerSettings properties can be set directly on a JsonSerializer instance. As an example, the code in figure 7-1 shows how you would set the Converters and NullValueHandling properties in a JsonSerializer object.

```
Figure 7-1

public void Go()
{
    var mySerializer = new JsonSerializer();
    mySerializer.Converters.Add(new JavaScriptDateTimeConverter());
    mySerializer.NullValueHandling = NullValueHandling.Ignore;
}
```

Since JsonSerializer reads and writes to streams, it can read/write directly to a file, or from an http request.

The code in figure 7-2 is going to serialize our Product class to a stream using JsonSerializer and then write the JSON to a text file. We've gone back to our basic Product class. Only Name and Stock are initialized in the ptodObj instance, so, by default, Sizes will contain null.

We instantiate our JsonSerializer and set NullValueHandling to ignore writing any null properties to the JSON. We also set Formatting to Indented so our JSON will be written in a "human readable" format.

Then we create a StreamWriter inside a using statement to ensure the stream is flushed and closed. The StreamWriter is set to write to a file named "product.json". We pass the StreamWriter to JsonTextWriter constructor, which accepts only a TextWriter object or derived class.

We then call the JsonSerializer Serialize() method, passing the prodObj to serialize, along with the JsonTextWriter object to write to.

```
Figure 7-2
public class Product
{
    public String Name { get; set; }
    public List<String> Sizes { get; set; }
    public int Stock { get; set; }
}
```

```
class Class1
{
    public void Go()
    {
        var prodObj = new Product()
        {
            Name = "Shirt",
            Stock = 5
        };

        var serializer = new JsonSerializer();
        serializer.NullValueHandling = NullValueHandling.Ignore;
        serializer.Formatting = Formatting.Indented;

        using (var sw = new StreamWriter(@"C:\product.json"))
        {
            using (var writer = new JsonTextWriter(sw))
            {
                serializer.Serialize(writer, prodObj);
            }
        }
    }
}
```

If we open product.json with a text editor, we would see the JSON shown in figure 7-3. Notice there is no Sizes property. Since it was null, the serializer setting for NullValueHandling prevented it from being written.

```
Figure 7-3

{
  "Name": "Shirt",
  "Stock": 5
}
```

This time we're going to read from a text file and deserialize it with JsonSerializer, as shown in figure 7-4. We use the same product.json file as source for the StreamReader, whose file contents appear in figure 7-3.

We start by instantiating a JsonSerializer object. Then we can set serializer options, if desired. For this demonstration, we instruct MissingMemberHandling to throw an error if the JSON contains elements that aren't in the deserialization class.

Then we call the Deserialize() method of the JsonSerializer, which takes either a JsonReader or TextReader derived class, and the deserialization class type. Since StreamReader derives from TextReader, well pass it to the deserializer method along with a Product type. The returned object ios then cast as Product to facilitate further use of the object.

```
Figure 7-4

public void Go()
{
    var serializer = new JsonSerializer();
    serializer.MissingMemberHandling = MissingMemberHandling.Error;

    using (StreamReader rdr = File.OpenText(@"C:\product.json"))
    {
        var prodObj = (Product)serializer.Deserialize(rdr,
                            typeof(Product));
    }
}
```

If we were to peek at the data of prodObj object, it would appear as shown in figure 7-5.

```
Figure 7-5

prodObj:
    Name        = "Shirt"
    Sizes       = null
    Stock       = 5
```

JsonSerializer works with all kinds of streams. You can even deserialize a stream straight from the web. Let's modify our Google Books API example, as seen in figure 7-6. We're going to get back the http response as a stream, pass it to a StreamReader and then send it to the JsonTextReader. The result is a fully populated Book object, from the class we defined in figure 2-12.

Don't forget to add a using directive for:

using System.Net.Http;

```
Figure 7-6

public void Go()
{
    var host = "https://www.googleapis.com";
    var url = host + "/books/v1/volumes?q=isbn:9780141314570";
    var serializer = new JsonSerializer();
    serializer.MissingMemberHandling = MissingMemberHandling.Ignore;

    var clientStream = new HttpClient();
    using (var stream = clientStream.GetStreamAsync(url).Result)
    {
        using (var streamReader = new StreamReader(stream))
        {
            using (var jsonReader = new JsonTextReader(streamReader))
```

```
            {
                var book = serializer.Deserialize<Book>(jsonReader);
            }
        }
    }
}
```

Notice a subtle difference in the JsonSerializer Deserialize() method between figure 7-4 and figure 7-6. In figure 7-6, we used an overload of the Deserialize() method with generic type parameters: Deserialize<Book>(jsonReader). This overload allows us to specify the return type (no casting required), but accepts only a JsonReader parameter (unlike the JsonConvert class, the method is not named DeserializeObject). In figure 7-4, we do not have a JsonReader object, we have a StreamReader, which derives from TextReader. Therefore, it must use the overload method that accepts a TextReader parameter. However, this version of the method returns an object, which must then be cast to the desired type.

As mentioned before, the JsonSerializer Deserialize() method is overloaded to accept either a JsonReader or TextReader derived class. Let's try passing the Deserialize() method a JsonTextReader (which derives from JsonReader). This will deserialize a JSON string instead of JSON from a stream, and is shown in figure 7-7.

The code starts off by defining a JSON product string. Next, it creates a JsonSerializer object and sets the MissingMemberHandling property. Since the JsonTextReader constructor only accepts a TextReader and not a JSON string, we must first pass the JSON string to the StringReader constructor (StringReader derives from TextReader).

```
Figure 7-7

public void Go()
{
    //sample source JSON
    var jsonStr = @"{
        ""Name"": ""Shirt"",
        ""Sizes"": [
          ""Small"",
          ""Medium""
        ],
        ""Stock"": 5
    }";

    var serializer = new JsonSerializer();
```

```
    serializer.MissingMemberHandling = MissingMemberHandling.Ignore;

    using (JsonReader jReader =
                        new JsonTextReader(new StringReader(jsonStr)))
    {
        var prodObj = serializer.Deserialize<Product>(jReader);
    }
}
```

Though for really large strings you should use a stream because any object over 85k goes on the Large Object Heap (LOH) in memory instead of the Small Object Heap (SOH). The LOH is not compacted due to the overhead of copying large chunks of memory. So it gets fragmented and could increase the memory footprint of your application. Json.NET uses streams to read portions at a time instead of loading the entire large string into memory.

```
{
    "Chapter" : "Eight",
    "Title" : [
                    "Linq to JSON",
                    "JToken",
                    "JObject",
                    "JArray"
              ]
}
```

Linq to JSON is an API for working with JSON objects. It resides in the Newtonsoft.Json.Linq namespace. The important classes in the namespace are: JObject, JArray, JValue, and JProperty. A majority of the classes inherit from the abstract classes JContainer or JToken.

The Linq to JSON hierarchy breaks down like this:

JToken	- abstract base class
JValue	- contains primitives (string, number, boolean, null)
JContainer	- abstract base class
JArray	- contains JTokens
JObject	- contains JProperties
JProperty	- contains objects with name (key) and JToken values

As mentioned in a previous chapter, a JSON object is denoted by curly braces: {}. A JSON array is denoted by square brackets: []. This is important when you consider a JSON object would be deserialized into a JObject; and a JSON array would be serialized into a JArray. A primitive value, however, would be deserialized into a JValue object.

JValue

A JValue object can store many kinds of primitive values (string, number, boolean, null). Consequently, the JValue class has many overloaded constructors so you can manually create a JValue object by passing it just about any type. For example, in figure 8-1, we create a JValue object by passing it an integer value. Notice in the second line, that the "Type" property of the JValue object holds the data type of the *value* (which in our case is Integer), but the *object's* type, from line three, is still a JValue. You can always check the Type property to cast the value to its appropriate type.

There are a few ways to extract the value contained in the JValue object. The first is to use the ToObject() method with a generic type parameter of <int>. Another way is to simply cast the entire object to int. And a third way is just to use the Value property. However, if you are unaware of the object type, you can always cast to JToken, since all the aforementioned classes inherit from JToken anyway.

```
Figure 8-1

var jval = new JValue(345);
var jvalValueType = jval.Type; //Integer
var jvalType = jval.GetType().Name; //JValue
```

```
//three ways to get value
var val1 = jval.ToObject<int>();
var val2 = (int)jval;
var val3 = jval.Value;
```

JProperty

A JProperty object (not to be confused with the JsonProperty attribute from chapter four) contains a single JToken in the Value field, paired with a Name field. Its other properties are inherited or overridden from either JContainer or JToken.

If you manually create a JProperty, you can only add it to JObject, as demonstrated in figure 8-2. In the first line, we create a JObject with one JProperty, which we assign a Name of "Name" and a Value of "Shirt". On line two, we add another JProperty, this one an integer value, using JObject's Add() method. It is interesting to note that both the string and integer literals are added to JProperty as JToken values.

```
Figure 8-2

public void Go()
{
    //create JObject with one JProperty
    var jObj = new JObject(new JProperty("Name", "Shirt"));

    //add a second JProperty
    jObj.Add(new JProperty("Stock", 5));
}
```

JObject

The code in figure 8-3 demonstrates how to iterate over a JObject with a foreach loop by casting it to the base class JToken and handling the JProperty objects. For this example, we go back to our Google Books API code. The code in figure 8-3 starts by fetching the JSON using HttpClient, saving it to the jsonStr variable, which is then deserialized to the Book class from figure 2-12. Actually, the code uses embedded foreach loops since, technically, the element book["items"] is a JArray that could contain multiple items, even though our simple example contains only a single book.

It is the inner foreach loop that we want to focus on, since this is where we iterate over the JObject. As you can see, the JObject is first cast to a JToken so that we can access each item as individual JProperty objects. The loop checks the Name of each JProperty to see if it equals volumeInfo. Remember that the Value portion of a JProperty contains a JToken, which is converted to a string with the generic Value() method.

```
Figure 8-3

public void Go()
{
    var jsonStr = string.Empty;
    var host = "https://www.googleapis.com";
    var url = host + "/books/v1/volumes?q=isbn:9780141314570";
    //first we make a call to the API
    using (var client = new HttpClient())
    {
        var response = client.GetAsync(url).Result;
        jsonStr = response.Content.ReadAsStringAsync().Result;
    }
    //deserialize the JSON to our Book class
    var book = JsonConvert.DeserializeObject<JObject>(jsonStr);

    //get title looping through JObject
    foreach (JObject obj in (JArray)book["items"])
    {
        foreach (JProperty jProp in (JToken)obj)
        {
            if (jProp.Name == "volumeInfo")
            {
                JToken jTok = jProp.Value;
                var title = jTok.Value<string>("title");
                break;
            }
        }
    }
}
```

Actually, you don't have to cast JObject to JToken just to access JProperty. There is another way. As shown in figure 8-4, you can simply call the Properties() method of the JObject, which returns the object's JProperty collection.

```
Figure 8-4

foreach (JProperty jProp in obj.Properties())
{
    if (jProp.Name == "volumeInfo")
    {
        JToken jTok = jProp.Value;
        var title = jTok.Value<string>("title");
        break;
    }
}
```

JObject Parse()

If your JSON source is a string (whether read from a file or fetched via API) JToken, JObject and JArray all have a Parse() method that will convert that string into the desired Json.NET object, as shown in figure 8-5. This is a quick and handy way to convert JSON into a JObject, JArray or JToken for further manipulation.

```
Figure 8-5

JObject obj = JObject.Parse(jsonStr);
JArray obj = JArray.Parse(jsonStr);
JToken obj = JToken.Parse(jsonStr);
```

JObject FromObject()

In figure 8-2, we manually created a JObject by using the "new" keyword. You can also create a JObject by *converting* an existing object. In figure 8-6, we create a JObject from a product object using the FromObject() method. The FromObject() method is really just a wrapper for the JsonSerializer class, and reuses its logic, except that a serializer is writing to a JsonTokenWriter instead of a JsonTextWriter.

```
Figure 8-6

public void Go()
{
    Product prod = new Product() { Name = "Shirt" };

    JObject prodObj = JObject.FromObject(prod);
}
```

Additionally, the FromObject() method comes in really handy for creating a JObject from an anonymous type, as show in figure 8-7. This is great for those times when creating a .NET class would be overkill.

```
Figure 8-7

public void Go()
{
    JObject prodObj = JObject.FromObject(new
    {
        Name = "Shirt",
        Stock = 5,
        Sizes = new String[] {"Large", "Medium"}
    });
}
```

Linq to JSON Queries

There are quite a few ways to get data using Linq to JSON: index notation, Children() method, SelectToken, SelectToken with JSONPath query, SelectToken with Linq Standard Query Operators. We will take a look at all of them.

For our Linq to JSON examples, we're going to use the Google Books API so we can work with a bit more complex JSON source, which we will then deserialize into a JObject.

Index Notation

The simplest way to get a value from Linq to Json is to use index notation on JObject/JArray. In figure 8-8, the code requests JSON from the Google Books API and deserializes the JSON to a JObject. From there, as shown in the last line, you can quickly get data by property name (if an object) or index (if a collection). This will return a JValue which can then be cast to a string. After running this code, the title variable will contain the string "The Outsiders".

```
Figure 8-8

public void Go()
{
    var jsonStr = string.Empty;
    var host = "https://www.googleapis.com";
    var url = host + "/books/v1/volumes?q=isbn:9780141314570";
    //first we make a call to the API
    using (var client = new HttpClient())
    {
        var response = client.GetAsync(url).Result;
        jsonStr = response.Content.ReadAsStringAsync().Result;
    }
    //deserialize the JSON to our Book class
    var book = JsonConvert.DeserializeObject<JObject>(jsonStr);

    var title = (string)book["items"][0]["volumeInfo"]["title"];
}
```

Children() method

JToken, JObject and JArray all have a Children() method that will return all the children values of a JObject/JArray as an IEnumerable<JToken>. If you include a using directive for System.Linq, then the collection can be queried using all the handy Linq standard query operators like Where(), OrderBy(), Select(), Sum(), etc. In figure 8-9, after fetching and deserializing the JSON, we use the Children() method to get all the child properties under the items element (see figure 2-11 for the JSON). Next, Linq standard query operators are used to get the book title. The next code statements show another option, using the Enumerable ElementAt() method to get the volumeInfo data. Linq then retrieves the book title from the volInfo object.

```
Figure 8-9

public void Go()
{
    var jsonStr = string.Empty;
    var host = "https://www.googleapis.com";
    var url = host + "/books/v1/volumes?q=isbn:9780141314570";
    //first we make a call to the API
    using (var client = new HttpClient())
    {
        var response = client.GetAsync(url).Result;
        jsonStr = response.Content.ReadAsStringAsync().Result;
    }
    //deserialize the JSON to our Book class
    var book = JsonConvert.DeserializeObject<JObject>(jsonStr);

    //get items
    var items = book["items"].Children();
    var title = (string)items
            .Select(p => p["volumeInfo"]["title"]).FirstOrDefault();

    //get volumeInfo via ElementAt()
    var volInfo = items.First().ElementAt(4);
    var title2 =
            (string)volInfo.Select(p => p["title"]).FirstOrDefault();
}
```

Notice, in figures 8-8 and 8-9, that we explicitly cast the returned JValue to a string for the title variable. But in figure 8-10, we instead take a two-step approach by first extracting the JValue object and assigning it to the titleJV variable. From there, we can either call the ToString() method or the Value() method with a generic type parameter of <string>.

```
Figure 8-10

var titleJV = book["items"]
    .Select(p => p["volumeInfo"]["title"]).FirstOrDefault();
if (titleJV != null)
{
    var title3 = titleJV.ToString();
    //or...
    var title4 = titleJV.Value<string();
}
```

SelectToken

We can also use the SelectToken() method to fetch data from the JObject, as shown in the last line of figure 8-11. You simply pass the entire path as a string parameter. What I like about using SelectToken() is that it doesn't throw an exception if the path is not valid. So, if any of the properties in the path are missing or misspelled, it would simply return null instead of throwing an exception. After running this code, the title variable would contain "The Outsiders", as expected.

```
Figure 8-11

public void Go()
{
    var jsonStr = string.Empty;
    var host = "https://www.googleapis.com";
    var url = host + "/books/v1/volumes?q=isbn:9780141314570";
    //first we make a call to the API
    using (var client = new HttpClient())
    {
        var response = client.GetAsync(url).Result;
        jsonStr = response.Content.ReadAsStringAsync().Result;
    }
    //deserialize the JSON to our Book class
    var book = JsonConvert.DeserializeObject<JObject>(jsonStr);

    //get title using path in SelectToken
    var title =
            (string)book.SelectToken("items[0].volumeInfo.title");
}
```

Of course, if we *wanted* to throw an exception if the path is invalid (no match found), that is easy, too. The SelectToken() method has an overload that accepts an "errorWhenNoMatch" boolean. In figure 8-12, the path in the first SelectToken() method specifies the 6th item in the "Item" array. Unfortunately, the JSON source only contains a single item in the array, so obviously, this path is not valid and no item will be found. By default, no exception would be thrown and the title variable would simply contain null. However, if we pass true for the errorWhenNoMatch parameter, as was done with the *second* call to the SelectToken() method, a JsonException would then be thrown.

```
Figure 8-12

public void Go()
{
    var jsonStr = string.Empty;
```

```
    var host = "https://www.googleapis.com";
    var url = host + "/books/v1/volumes?q=isbn:9780141314570";
    //first we make a call to the API
    using (var client = new HttpClient())
    {
        var response = client.GetAsync(url).Result;
        jsonStr = response.Content.ReadAsStringAsync().Result;
    }
    //deserialize the JSON to our Book class
    var book = JsonConvert.DeserializeObject<JObject>(jsonStr);

    //title will contain null
    var title =
            (string)book.SelectToken("items[5].volumeInfo.title");

    //setting errorWhenNoMatch to true would throw a JsonException
    var title2 =
        (string)book.SelectToken("items[5].volumeInfo.title", true);
}
```

In addition to passing the SelectToken() method a string path to the child tokens, you can also pass JSONPath queries or Linq standard query operators (extension methods with lambda expressions). Let's take a quick look at how to do both of these.

SelectToken with JSONPath

JSONPath is a syntax for querying JSON as a tree of nodes. I will cover a few JSONPath basics, but if you need more detailed information on JSONPath, just go to goessner.net.

The root node operator in JSONPath is represented by a $ sign. It will return all the nodes inside the JSON document. To get the children of a given node, you can use either the dot (.) operator or square brackets []. For example, $.products and $['Products'] would return the same thing.

The asterisk * is a wild card character that returns everything in the node. For example, to return all the items in a Products, object use: $.Products[*].Items or $['Products'][*].Items

You can also use array index, starting at zero: $.Products[0] or $['Products'][0]

To get specific items in the array, you can use the slicer operator in the format of [StartIndex : EndIndex : Steps]. For example, you could use: $..Products[4,8,2] or

$..['Products'][4,8,2] The double dot performs recursive descent and selects all matching child nodes no matter where they are.

Filter expressions can be used to filter the arrays: ['Products'][?(<expression>)], but they must evaluate to a boolean. For example, ['Products'][?(@.stock > 18)] where @ represents the current item in the array being processed.

Now that we know some JSONPath basics, let's use it to extract the book title from the Google API JSON. In figure 8-13, the last three lines of the code calls the SelectToken() method with different JSONPath string. All three JSONPath examples return the same thing, the string: "The Outsiders".

```
Figure 8-13

public void Go()
{
    var jsonStr = string.Empty;
    var host = "https://www.googleapis.com";
    var url = host + "/books/v1/volumes?q=isbn:9780141314570";
    //first we make a call to the API
    using (var client = new HttpClient())
    {
        var response = client.GetAsync(url).Result;
        jsonStr = response.Content.ReadAsStringAsync().Result;
    }
    //deserialize the JSON to our Book class
    var book = JsonConvert.DeserializeObject<JObject>(jsonStr);

    //get title using JSONPath in SelectToken
    var title1 = (string)book.SelectToken("$..title");
    var title2 =
          (string)book.SelectToken("$.items[0].volumeInfo.title");
    var title3 =
          (string)book.SelectToken("$.items[-1:].volumeInfo.title");
}
```

SelectToken with Linq Standard Query Operators

The code in figure 8-14 demonstrates how to use the SelectToken() method with Linq standard query operators, which are extension methods with a lambda expression. In the last line of code, the SelectToken() method is called, and then chained with the Linq standard query operators Select() and FirstOrDefault().

```
Figure 8-14

public void Go()
{
    var jsonStr = string.Empty;
    var host = "https://www.googleapis.com";
    var url = host + "/books/v1/volumes?q=isbn:9780141314570";
    //first we make a call to the API
    using (var client = new HttpClient())
    {
        var response = client.GetAsync(url).Result;
        jsonStr = response.Content.ReadAsStringAsync().Result;
    }
    //deserialize the JSON to our Book class
    var book = JsonConvert.DeserializeObject<JObject>(jsonStr);

    //get title using linq standard query operators
    var title = book.SelectToken("items").Select(p =>
            (string)p["volumeInfo"]["title"]).FirstOrDefault();
}
```

Serialize Partial JSON

Another good use of Linq to JSON is extracting only the pieces of the JSON data you are interested in. This is especially handy when consuming third-party APIs that return a huge and complex JSON payload, when all you are interested in are a few bits of data for use on your web page. Using Linq to JSON to extract theses JSON fragments also allows you to define a smaller number of .NET classes to hold just the data you need, as opposed to designing multiple complex classes to accommodate the entire JSON payload. As a result, you are passing the Json.NET serializer only the JSON you want, and not the whole entire JSON payload.

In previous examples, we consumed JSON from the Google Books API. The JSON it returned contained many objects and properties, but we were only interested in a few keys details about a book, such as title and author. This is a perfect example to use Ling to JSON to extract only the data we need.

For example, suppose we wanted to get a list of all the book names written by S.E. Hinton. If we call the Google Books API and request all the books by S.E. Hinton, it would return quite a bit of data. Figure 8-15 shows an *abbreviated* version of the JSON payload, listing just two of the ten S.E. Hinton books on record.

Figure 8-15


```
{
  "kind": "books#volumes",
  "totalItems": 95,
  "items": [
    {
      "kind": "books#volume",
      "id": "y9r_uY0EGmkC",
      "etag": "ibAcyciXBfk",
      "selfLink":
"https://www.googleapis.com/books/v1/volumes/y9r_uY0EGmkC",
      "volumeInfo": {
        "title": "That Was Then, This Is Now",
        "authors": [
          "S. E. Hinton"
        ],
        "publisher": "Penguin",
        "publishedDate": "2012-05-15",
        "description": "Another classic from the author of the
internationally bestselling The Outsiders Continue celebrating 50
years of The Outsiders by reading this companion novel. That Was
Then, This is Now is S. E. Hinton's moving portrait of the bond
between best friends Bryon and Mark and the tensions that develop
between them as they begin to grow up and grow apart. \"A mature,
disciplined novel which excites a response in the reader . . . Hard
to forget.\"—The New York Times",
        "industryIdentifiers": [
          {
            "type": "ISBN_13",
            "identifier": "9781101642597"
          },
          {
            "type": "ISBN_10",
            "identifier": "1101642599"
          }
        ],
        "readingModes": {
          "text": true,
          "image": false
        },
        "pageCount": 160,
        "printType": "BOOK",
        "categories": [
          "Young Adult Fiction"
        ],
        "averageRating": 4.0,
        "ratingsCount": 39,
        "maturityRating": "NOT_MATURE",
        "allowAnonLogging": true,
        "contentVersion": "1.3.2.0.preview.2",
        "panelizationSummary": {
          "containsEpubBubbles": false,
          "containsImageBubbles": false
        },
        "imageLinks": {
          "smallThumbnail":
"http://books.google.com/books/content?id=y9r_uY0EGmkC&printsec=fron
```

```
tcover&img=1&zoom=5&edge=curl&source=gbs_api",
          "thumbnail":
"http://books.google.com/books/content?id=y9r_uY0EGmkC&printsec=fron
tcover&img=1&zoom=1&edge=curl&source=gbs_api"
        },
        "language": "en",
        "previewLink":
"http://books.google.com/books?id=y9r_uY0EGmkC&printsec=frontcover&d
q=inauthor:SE+Hinton&hl=&cd=7&source=gbs_api",
        "infoLink":
"https://play.google.com/store/books/details?id=y9r_uY0EGmkC&source=
gbs_api",
        "canonicalVolumeLink":
"https://market.android.com/details?id=book-y9r_uY0EGmkC"
      },
      "saleInfo": {
        "country": "US",
        "saleability": "FOR_SALE",
        "isEbook": true,
        "listPrice": {
          "amount": 9.99,
          "currencyCode": "USD"
        },
        "retailPrice": {
          "amount": 9.99,
          "currencyCode": "USD"
        },
        "buyLink":
"https://play.google.com/store/books/details?id=y9r_uY0EGmkC&rdid=bo
ok-y9r_uY0EGmkC&rdot=1&source=gbs_api",
        "offers": [
          {
            "finskyOfferType": 1,
            "listPrice": {
              "amountInMicros": 9990000.0,
              "currencyCode": "USD"
            },
            "retailPrice": {
              "amountInMicros": 9990000.0,
              "currencyCode": "USD"
            },
            "giftable": true
          }
        ]
      },
      "accessInfo": {
        "country": "US",
        "viewability": "PARTIAL",
        "embeddable": true,
        "publicDomain": false,
        "textToSpeechPermission": "ALLOWED_FOR_ACCESSIBILITY",
        "epub": {
          "isAvailable": true,
          "acsTokenLink":
"http://books.google.com/books/download/That_Was_Then_This_Is_Now-
sample-
epub.acsm?id=y9r_uY0EGmkC&format=epub&output=acs4_fulfillment_token&
dl_type=sample&source=gbs_api"
```

```
        },
        "pdf": {
          "isAvailable": false
        },
        "webReaderLink":
"http://play.google.com/books/reader?id=y9r_uY0EGmkC&hl=&printsec=frontcover&source=gbs_api",
        "accessViewStatus": "SAMPLE",
        "quoteSharingAllowed": false
      },
      "searchInfo": {
        "textSnippet": "That Was Then, This is Now is S. E. Hinton&#39;s moving portrait of the bond between best friends Bryon and Mark and the tensions that develop between them as they begin to grow up and grow apart."
      }
    },
    {
      "kind": "books#volume",
      "id": "VSRQAAAAYAAJ",
      "etag": "PBgKleJIWo8",
      "selfLink":
"https://www.googleapis.com/books/v1/volumes/VSRQAAAAYAAJ",
      "volumeInfo": {
        "title": "The Outsiders",
        "subtitle": "That was Then, this is Now ; Rumble Fish",
        "authors": [
          "S. E. Hinton"
        ],
        "publishedDate": "1995",
        "industryIdentifiers": [
          {
            "type": "OTHER",
            "identifier": "UVA:X004780566"
          }
        ],
        "readingModes": {
          "text": false,
          "image": false
        },
        "pageCount": 447,
        "printType": "BOOK",
        "categories": [
          "Brothers"
        ],
        "maturityRating": "NOT_MATURE",
        "allowAnonLogging": false,
        "contentVersion": "0.0.1.0.preview.0",
        "imageLinks": {
          "smallThumbnail":
"http://books.google.com/books/content?id=VSRQAAAAYAAJ&printsec=frontcover&img=1&zoom=5&source=gbs_api",
          "thumbnail":
"http://books.google.com/books/content?id=VSRQAAAAYAAJ&printsec=frontcover&img=1&zoom=1&source=gbs_api"
        },
        "language": "en",
        "previewLink":
```

```
"http://books.google.com/books?id=VSRQAAAAYAAJ&q=inauthor:SE+Hinton&
dq=inauthor:SE+Hinton&hl=&cd=10&source=gbs_api",
        "infoLink":
"http://books.google.com/books?id=VSRQAAAAYAAJ&dq=inauthor:SE+Hinton
&hl=&source=gbs_api",
        "canonicalVolumeLink":
"https://books.google.com/books/about/The_Outsiders.html?hl=&id=VSRQ
AAAAYAAJ"
      },
      "saleInfo": {
        "country": "US",
        "saleability": "NOT_FOR_SALE",
        "isEbook": false
      },
      "accessInfo": {
        "country": "US",
        "viewability": "NO_PAGES",
        "embeddable": false,
        "publicDomain": false,
        "textToSpeechPermission": "ALLOWED",
        "epub": {
          "isAvailable": false
        },
        "pdf": {
          "isAvailable": false
        },
        "webReaderLink":
"http://play.google.com/books/reader?id=VSRQAAAAYAAJ&hl=&printsec=fr
ontcover&source=gbs_api",
        "accessViewStatus": "NONE",
        "quoteSharingAllowed": false
      }
    }
  ]
}
```

Yikes! That is a lot of JSON data. You can see why we don't want to build classes for the entire payload. After inspecting the JSON, we realize we are only interested in the multiple volumeInfo objects in the items array. Let's use Linq to JSON to extract just those objects. First, we'll create a few classes to hold the data in volumeInfo, as shown in figure 8-16. VolumeInfo is created as the parent class. Notice we only had to create four classes to hold the volumeInfo JSON fragment, instead of the seventeen classes we would have needed had we deserialized the entire JSON payload!

```
Figure 8-16

public class Volumeinfo
{
    public string title { get; set; }
    public string[] authors { get; set; }
    public string publisher { get; set; }
```

```
    public string publishedDate { get; set; }
    public string description { get; set; }
    public Industryidentifier[] industryIdentifiers { get; set; }
    public Readingmodes readingModes { get; set; }
    public int pageCount { get; set; }
    public string printType { get; set; }
    public string[] categories { get; set; }
    public float averageRating { get; set; }
    public int ratingsCount { get; set; }
    public string maturityRating { get; set; }
    public bool allowAnonLogging { get; set; }
    public string contentVersion { get; set; }
    public Imagelinks imageLinks { get; set; }
    public string language { get; set; }
    public string previewLink { get; set; }
    public string infoLink { get; set; }
    public string canonicalVolumeLink { get; set; }
}

public class Readingmodes
{
    public bool text { get; set; }
    public bool image { get; set; }
}

public class Imagelinks
{
    public string smallThumbnail { get; set; }
    public string thumbnail { get; set; }
}

public class Industryidentifier
{
    public string type { get; set; }
    public string identifier { get; set; }
}
```

Now we'll look at the code in figure 8-17, which calls the API and extracts the desired JSON fragment. The code begins the same way as our previous examples, it builds the url, calls the Google API, and parses the JSON into a JObject named bookObj that we will use to query.

We use the Children() method to grab all the volumeInfo objects and return it as a list of JTokens (JObject inherits the Children() method from JContainer, which overrides the same method in JToken).

Then we iterate over the list of JToken with a foreach loop. Each JToken item contains one volumeInfo element from the JSON. It gets converted to a VolumeInfo class object by calling the ToObject<VolumeInfo>() generic method. We then add each newly created VolumeInfo object to a list of VolumeInfo objects.

```
Figure 8-17

public class Class1
{
    public void Go()
    {
        var jsonStr = string.Empty;
        var host = "https://www.googleapis.com";
        var url = host + "/books/v1/volumes?q=inauthor:SE+Hinton";

        //first we make a call to the API
        using (var client = new HttpClient())
        {
            var response = client.GetAsync(url).Result;
            jsonStr = response.Content.ReadAsStringAsync().Result;
        }

        //convert the JSON string into a JObject
        var bookObj = JObject.Parse(jsonStr);

        //extract volumeInfo objects into a list
        List<JToken> volumeInfoList =
                bookObj["items"].Children()["volumeInfo"].ToList();

        //serialize into Volumeinfo objects
        var volumeList = new List<Volumeinfo>();
        foreach (JToken volumeInfoToken in volumeInfoList)
        {
            //JToken.ToObject will use JsonSerializer internally
            var volumeInfo = volumeInfoToken.ToObject<Volumeinfo>();
            volumeList.Add(volumeInfo);
        }

        //output list of book titles
        foreach (Volumeinfo vi in volumeList)
        {
            Console.WriteLine(vi.title);
        }
    }
}
```

Finally, the code iterates over the list of VolumeInfo objects and writes the title of each book to the console window. The output of the program is displayed in figure 8-18. The "Untitled Hinton Book" just proves that not even Google's API data is 100% clean.

```
Figure 8-18

Hawkes Harbor
S.E. Hinton Classic Collection
The Outsiders
```

```
S. E. Hinton's the Puppy Sister
Rumble Fish
Tex
That Was Then, This Is Now
Some of Tim's Stories
Untitled Hinton Book
The Outsiders
```

I'm sure you'll agree that it is a lot easier and more efficient to use Linq to JSON to process just the JSON you need. That's where Linq to JSON really comes in handy.

JSON Merge

The abstract JContainer class contains a handy Merge() method for combining two JSON objects or two JSON arrays. The Merge() method is inherited by the JObject, JArray and JProperty classes. However, the Merge() method in the parent JContainer class does little more than call an internal abstract method named MergeMethod(). Therefore, classes derived from JContainer (JObject, JArray, JProperty) must override MergeMethod() and provide custom logic to merge data tailored to their unique class structure.

The bottom line is, Json.NET provides the ability to merge two JSON objects or two JSON arrays. This can be very handy in a variety of circumstances. But that's not all. The Merge() method is overloaded to accept a JsonMergeSettings object. It contains a MergeArrayHandling property that lets you specify *how* JSON array items are merged. The MergeArrayHandling property can be set to one of four enum values: Union, Replace, Merge, and Concat.

"Union" will eliminate duplicate array items. "Replace" will replace all the items in the first array with items from the second array. "Merge" will replace array items by index position, that is, item 1 of the first array will be replaced with item 1 from the second array, and so on. "Concat" will concatenate arrays, that is to say, all the items in the second array will be *added* to the first array.

The JsonMergeSettings object also contains a MergeNullValueHandling property which can be set to one of two enum values to specify how nulls are handled. Nulls can either be Merged or Ignored. That seems self-explanatory, so let's focus our attention on using the MergeArrayHandling property.

Concat Merge Array

Let's take a look at how to merge JSON using the Concat method. Referring to the code in figure 8-19, we create two product JObject's using JObject.Parse() with a JSON string. Notice both JSON strings contain an array of different sizes. Actually, the Sizes array is the element we will focus on when highlighting the merging differences among the four MergeArrayHandling options. The prod1 Sizes array contains two items, while the prod2 Sizes array contains three items.

Next, we call the Merge() method of prod1, passing it the prod2 object and a JsonMergeSettings object with the MergeArrayHandling property set to Concat. This merges the data of prod2 to prod1. Finally, we assign the merged JSON of prod1 to the jsonStr variable so we can inspect the result.

```
Figure 8-19

public void Go()
{
    var prod1 = JObject.Parse(@"{
        ""Name"": ""Shirt"",
        ""Stock"": ""5"",
        ""Sizes"": [
            ""Large"",
            ""Medium""
        ],
        ""Price"": 21.99
    }");

    var prod2 = JObject.Parse(@"{
        ""Stock"": ""9"",
        ""Sizes"": [
            ""Small"",
            ""Medium"",
            ""Extra Large""
        ],
        ""UPC"": ""123456789"",
        ""Price"": 19.99
    }");

    prod1.Merge(prod2, new JsonMergeSettings
    {
        MergeArrayHandling = MergeArrayHandling.Concat
    });

    var jsonStr = prod1.ToString();
}
```

The contents of the jsonStr variable appears in figure 8-20. Since prod1 is a JObject and not a JArray, let's first consider the effects of the JObject.Merge()

method. Notice the value of Stock in the final JSON is "9" instead of its original value of "5". During the merge, the Stock value from prod2 overwrote the Stock value of prod1. Same thing happened with Price. The value of 21.99 from prod1 was overwritten with the value of 19.99 from prod2. Another interesting thing to note, is that only prod2 contained UPC, so it was added to prod1 during the merge.

The result of setting the MergeArrayHandling property to Concat becomes apparent with the Sizes array. The prod1 Sizes array originally contained two items, while the prod2 Sizes array contained three items. The result of a Concat merge is that the Sizes array now contains all five items, including duplicates of the "Medium" item, which was contained in both Sizes array.

Figure 8-20

```
{
  "Name": "Shirt",
  "Stock": "9",
  "Sizes": [
    "Large",
    "Medium",
    "Small",
    "Medium",
    "Extra Large"
  ],
  "Price": 19.99,
  "UPC": "123456789"
}
```

Union Merge Array

What if we don't want duplicate values in our array? Then we can set the MergeArrayHandling property of the JsonMergeSettings object to Union, as was done in figure 8-21.

Figure 8-21

```
prod1.Merge(prod2, new JsonMergeSettings
{
    MergeArrayHandling = MergeArrayHandling.Union
});
```

This time when the code is run, the resulting JSON appears in figure 8-22. Everything appears the same except the Sizes array now only contains four items. The duplicate Medium item was eliminated.

```
Figure 8-22

{
  "Name": "Shirt",
  "Stock": "9",
  "Sizes": [
    "Large",
    "Medium",
    "Small",
    "Extra Large"
  ],
  "Price": 19.99,
  "UPC": "123456789"
}
```

Replace Merge Array

The Replace option will replace all the items in the first array with items from the second array. For this demonstration we had to alter the JSON string source a little bit, as shown in figure 8-23. The prod1 Sizes array now contains only 1 item, “Large”, which is not in the prod2 Sizes array. The prod2 Sizes array contains three items, all of which are not in the prod1 Sizes array. Next, the MergeArrayHandling property in the JsonMergeSettings object is set to MergeArrayHandling.Replace.

```
Figure 8-23

public void Go()
{
    var prod1 = JObject.Parse(@"{
        ""Name"": ""Shirt"",
        ""Stock"": ""5"",
        ""Sizes"": [
            ""Large""
        ],
        ""Price"": 21.99
    }");

    var prod2 = JObject.Parse(@"{
        ""Stock"": ""9"",
        ""Sizes"": [
            ""Small"",
            ""Medium"",
            ""Extra Large""
        ],
        ""UPC"": ""123456789"",
        ""Price"": 19.99
    }");

    prod1.Merge(prod2, new JsonMergeSettings
    {
        MergeArrayHandling = MergeArrayHandling.Replace
    });
```

```
    var jsonStr = prod1.ToString();
}
```

When we run the code, the resulting JSON appears in figure 8-24. Notice the Sizes array no longer contains "Large" from the original prod1 object. It was completely replaced by the three items from the prod2 Sizes array.

```
Figure 8-24

{
  "Name": "Shirt",
  "Stock": "9",
  "Sizes": [
    "Small",
    "Medium",
    "Extra Large"
  ],
  "Price": 19.99,
  "UPC": "123456789"
}
```

Merge Array

The effects of the Merge option is a little more subtle, in that it replaces array items by index position. Item 1 of first array will be replaced by item 1 from 2nd array, and so on. To see this in action, we modified the prod1 JSON string again, as shown in figure 8-25. This time, the Sizes array contains "Large" at index 0, "Medium" at index 1, and “Extra Large” at index 2. The Sizes array in prod2 has just the opposite; "Medium" at index 0 and "Large" at index 1. This order of Sizes in prod2 just makes more sense. We also set the MergeArrayHandling property in the JsonMergeSettings object to MergeArrayHandling.Merge.

```
Figure 8-25

public void Go()
{
    var prod1 = JObject.Parse(@"{
        ""Name"": ""Shirt"",
        ""Stock"": ""5"",
        ""Sizes"": [
            ""Large"",
            ""Medium"",
            ""Extra Large""
        ],
        ""Price"": 21.99
    }");

    var prod2 = JObject.Parse(@"{
```

```
        ""Sizes"": [
            ""Medium"",
            ""Large""
        ],
        ""UPC"": ""123456789""
    }");

    prod1.Merge(prod2, new JsonMergeSettings
    {
        MergeArrayHandling = MergeArrayHandling.Merge
    });

    var jsonStr = prod1.ToString();
}
```

When we run the code, the resulting JSON appears in figure 8-26. Notice the Sizes array now has the sizes in correct order because the first two items from the prod1 Sizes array were overwritten by the first two items from the prod2 Sizes array. The "Large" of prod1 was replaced by "Medium" from prod2. The "Medium" of prod1 was replaced by the "Large" from prod2. The “Extra Large” of prod1 was unaffected since there was no item at index 2 in the prod2 Sizes array.

```
Figure 8-26

{
  "Name": "Shirt",
  "Stock": "5",
  "Sizes": [
    "Medium",
    "Large",
    "Extra Large"
  ],
  "Price": 21.99,
  "UPC": "123456789"
}
```

{

"Chapter" : "Nine", "Title" : "JSON Schema and Validation"

}

Json.NET Schema describes the structure of a JSON document, its required properties and length limitations. Your applications can use the schema to validate JSON. The JSON Schemas themselves are just JSON documents, described by a new media type "application/schema+json". The JSON document to which a schema has been applied is known as an "instance".

Json.NET Schema is a separate package and is not free, but there is a trial/limited version. You can read the spec by browsing to www.json-schema.org and clicking the Specifications link.

Json.NET Schema is installed by using NuGet. To install, launch a project in Visual Studio and open the NuGet Package Manager Console (details on using NuGet appear in Appendix A). At the command prompt, enter:

Install-Package Newtonsoft.Json.Schema

Let's dive in and generate a schema from our simple product class, as shown in figure 9-1. Don't forget to add a using directive for:

using Newtonsoft.Json.Schema.Generation;

```
Figure 9-1

class Class1
{
    public void Go()
    {
        var jSchemaGenerator = new JSchemaGenerator();
        var schema = jSchemaGenerator.Generate(typeof(Product));
        var schemaJson = schema.ToString();
    }
}

public class Product
{
    public string Name { get; set; }
    public int Stock { get; set; }
    public List<string> Sizes { get; set; }
}
```

The Product class remains relatively simple, for now. The code to generate a schema from a class is pretty simple, just three lines. First, a new JSchemaGenerator instance is created. Then we call its Generate() method, passing it the type of object to use to generate a schema from, in our case, Product. Lastly, since the schema is, in itself, a JSON document, we save the schema JSON to a variable.

The schema JSON contained in the schemaJson variable appears in figure 9-2. It has three root members, called keywords: type, properties and required. The "type" in our schema equals “object”, which means any JSON using this schema must be an object. The "properties" object contains an object for each of our three class properties: Name, Stock, Sizes. Each of these objects contains a type member specifying the property data type. Any items appearing in the "required" array means those properties must exist in any JSON using this schema.

```
Figure 9-2

{
  "type": "object",
  "properties": {
    "Name": {
      "type": [
```

```
        "string",
        "null"
      ]
    },
    "Stock": {
      "type": "integer"
    },
    "Sizes": {
      "type": [
        "array",
        "null"
      ],
      "items": {
        "type": [
          "string",
          "null"
        ]
      }
    }
  },
  "required": [
    "Name",
    "Stock",
    "Sizes"
  ]
}
```

If any class attributes or property attributes are defined, they will be included in the JSON schema. For example, we modified our Product class, as shown in figure 9-3, by adding some class attributes and some property attributes for DisplayName and Description. Don't forget to add a using directive for: using System.ComponentModel;

```
Figure 9-3

[DisplayName("Apparel Products")]
[Description("Products from the Apparel category")]
public class Product
{
    public string Name { get; set; }
    [DisplayName("Stock level")]
    [Description("number of items in inventory")]
    public int Stock { get; set; }
    public List<string> Sizes { get; set; }
}
```

This time, when we run the same Go() method from figure 9-1, the attribute data is included in the JSON schema output, as shown in figure 9-4. Notice we have two new members in the root level of the JSON: title and description. The title member contains the DisplayName attribute data that appeared over the Product class declaration. The description member contains the Description attribute data that appeared over the class declaration. The same two members, title and description, were also added to the Stock object to match the attributes over the property declaration.

```
Figure 9-4

{
  "title": "Apparel Products",
  "description": "Products from the Apparel category",
  "type": "object",
  "properties": {
    "Name": {
      "type": [
        "string",
        "null"
      ]
    },
    "Stock": {
      "title": "Stock level",
      "description": "number of items in inventory",
      "type": "integer"
    },
    "Sizes": {
      "type": [
        "array",
        "null"
      ],
      "items": {
        "type": [
          "string",
          "null"
        ]
      }
    }
  },
  "required": [
    "Name",
    "Stock",
    "Sizes"
  ]
}
```

ContractResolver

You can also set properties to customize how the schema is generated. For example, you can set the ContractResolver property to use camel casing for property names by using the built-in camel case ContractResolver. To illustrate this transformation, we modified the Product class with longer property names using

Pascal casing, as shown in figure 9-5. To use the camel case resolver, you may need to add a using directive for: using Newtonsoft.Json.Serialization;

In the Go() method, a new JSchemaGenerator is instantiated. In the resulting object, the ContractResolver property is assigned the camel case contact resolver. The schema is then generated with a call to the Generate() method, and the resulting JSON is saved to the schemaJson variable.

```
Figure 9-5

class Class1
{
    public void Go()
    {
        var jSchemaGenerator = new JSchemaGenerator();
        jSchemaGenerator.ContractResolver =
                       new CamelCasePropertyNamesContractResolver();
        var schema = jSchemaGenerator.Generate(typeof(Product));
        var schemaJson = schema.ToString();
    }
}

public class Product
{
    public string ProductName { get; set; }
    public int StockLevel { get; set; }
    public List<string> Sizes { get; set; }
}
```

After running the code, the contents of the schemaJson variable are shown in figure 9-6. Notice that the property names for ProductName and StockLevel have been changed to camel casing.

```
Figure 9-6

{
  "type": "object",
  "properties": {
    "productName": {
      "type": [
        "string",
        "null"
      ]
    },
    "stockLevel": {
      "type": "integer"
    },
    "sizes": {
      "type": [
        "array",
        "null"
      ],
      "items": {
```

```
          "type": [
            "string",
            "null"
          ]
        }
      }
    },
    "required": [
      "productName",
      "stockLevel",
      "sizes"
    ]
  }
```

Manual Schema Generation

You can also manually generate a schema from a JSON string, since a JSON schema is really just a JSON document. The code in figure 9-7 creates a JSON string schema similar to the format depicted in figure 9-6. Next, the JSON string is then converted into a JSchema object using the JSchema.Parse() method.

```
Figure 9-7

public void Go()
{
    var productSchemaStr = @"{
        ""type"": ""object"",
        ""properties"": {
        ""Name"": {
            ""type"": ""string""
        },
        ""Stock"": {
            ""type"": ""integer""
        },
        ""Sizes"": {
            ""type"": ""array"",
            ""items"": {
            ""type"": ""string""
            }
        }
        }
    }";

    var productSchema = JSchema.Parse(productSchemaStr);
}
```

You can also manually generate a schema using the JSchema class. In figure 9-8, we manually generate a JSON schema for our Product class. Using an object initializer, we construct a JSchema object and set the properties for Type and

Properties. Then we save the resulting JSON to the schemaJson variable. Don't forget to add a using directive for: using Newtonsoft.Json.Schema;

```
Figure 9-8

public void Go()
{
    var productSchema = new JSchema
    {
        Type = JSchemaType.Object,
        Properties = {
            { "Name", new JSchema { Type = JSchemaType.String } },
            { "Stock", new JSchema { Type = JSchemaType.Integer } },
            { "Sizes", new JSchema { Type = JSchemaType.Array,
                    Items =
                    {
                        new JSchema { Type = JSchemaType.String }
                    }
                }
            }
        }
    };

    var schemaJson = productSchema.ToString();
}
```

The JSON contents of the schemaJson variable appears in figure 9-9. Notice we don't have a "required" object in our JSON to mark members as required. So how do we tell Json.NET Schema to include a required object?

```
Figure 9-9

{
  "type": "object",
  "properties": {
    "Name": {
      "type": "string"
    },
    "Stock": {
      "type": "integer"
    },
    "Sizes": {
      "type": "array",
      "items": {
        "type": "string"
      }
    }
  }
}
```

If we tried to specify this within the object initializer of figure 9-8, such as adding: Required = Required.Default, we would get the compiler error "Property or indexer 'Required' cannot be assigned to -- it is read only". This is because the

JSchema Required property only has a getter, it doesn't have a setter. So we have to add any requirements after the object has been created, as shown in figure 9-10.

```
Figure 9-10

public void Go()
{
    var productSchema = new JSchema
    {
        Type = JSchemaType.Object,
        Properties =  {
            { "Name", new JSchema { Type = JSchemaType.String } },
            { "Stock", new JSchema { Type = JSchemaType.Number} },
            { "Sizes", new JSchema{
                    Type = JSchemaType.Array,
                    Items = {
                        new JSchema { Type = JSchemaType.String }
                    }
                }
            }
        }
    };
    //add required properties
    productSchema.Required.Add("Name");
    productSchema.Required.Add("Stock");
    productSchema.Required.Add("Sizes");

    var schemaJson = productSchema.ToString();
}
```

This time when we run the code, the resulting JSON contains a required object, as shown in figure 9-11.

```
Figure 9-11

{
  "type": "object",
  "properties": {
    "Name": {
      "type": "string"
    },
    "Stock": {
      "type": "number"
    },
    "Sizes": {
      "type": "array",
      "items": {
        "type": "string"
      }
    }
  },
  "required": [
    "Name",
    "Stock",
    "Sizes"
  ]
}
```

Validation

Now that we know how to generate a Json.NET schema, let's see how to use it to validate a JSON object. In the code in figure 9-12, we create our productSchema object with a JSchema object initializer. Then we add required fields for Name, Stock and Sizes. Next, we use JObject.Parse() to turn a JSON product string into a JObject prodObj. To validate the Product object against the schema, all we have to do is call the prodObj's IsValid() method, passing it the productSchema as the schema to validate against. Both JObject and JArray have an IsValid() instance method.

Figure 9-12

```
public void Go()
{
    //manually generate the schema
    var productSchema = new JSchema
    {
        Type = JSchemaType.Object,
        Properties = {
            { "Name", new JSchema { Type = JSchemaType.String } },
            { "Stock", new JSchema { Type = JSchemaType.Integer } },
            { "Sizes", new JSchema{
                    Type = JSchemaType.Array,
                    Items = {
                        new JSchema { Type = JSchemaType.String }
                    }
                }
            }
        }
    };

    //add required properties
    productSchema.Required.Add("Name");
    productSchema.Required.Add("Stock");
    productSchema.Required.Add("Sizes");

    //create JObject from source JSON
    var prodJObj = JObject.Parse(@"
    {
        ""Name"": ""Shirt"",
        ""Sizes"": [""Medium"", ""Large""],
        ""Stock"": 5,
        ""UPC"": ""123456789""
    }");

    //validate against schema
    bool isValid = prodJObj.IsValid(productSchema);
}
```

After running the code in figure 9-12, the isValid boolean would contain true.

Now let's see what would happen if our JSON object failed schema validation. In figure 9-13, let's omit the Stock member from the product JSON string passed to the JObject.Parse() method to force a failed validation. Now we just need a way to view the error messages. An overload for the IsValid() method accepts an out parameter of a list of strings. Any error messages will be added to this list. The last three lines in the code below declares such a list and passes it to the IsValid() method. Any error messages are then saved to the errorMessages variable.

```
Figure 9-13

public void Go()
{
    //manually generate the schema
    var productSchema = new JSchema
    {
        Type = JSchemaType.Object,
        Properties = {
            { "Name", new JSchema { Type = JSchemaType.String } },
            { "Stock", new JSchema { Type = JSchemaType.Integer } },
            { "Sizes", new JSchema{
                    Type = JSchemaType.Array,
                    Items = {
                        new JSchema { Type = JSchemaType.String }
                    }
                }
            }
        }
    };

    //add required properties
    productSchema.Required.Add("Name");
    productSchema.Required.Add("Stock");
    productSchema.Required.Add("Sizes");

    //create JObject from source JSON
    var prodJObj = JObject.Parse(@"
    {
        ""Name"": ""Shirt"",
        ""Sizes"": [""Medium"", ""Large""],
        ""UPC"": ""123456789""
    }");

    //validate against schema
    IList<string> errorsList;
    bool isValid = prodJObj.IsValid(productSchema, out errorsList);
    var errorMessages = String.Join(";", errorsList.ToArray());
}
```

When this code is run, the isValid boolean will contain false because Stock is missing from the source JSON yet it is required by the schema. As a result, the contents of the errorMessages variable will be: "Required properties are missing from object: Stock. Path '', line 2, position 13".

Internally, the IsValid() method uses the JSchemaValidatingReader class to perform validation. So if we wanted to perform validation while *reading* JSON, we can use the JSchemaValidatingReader class directly. To validate while *writing* JSON, we would use the JSchemaValidatingWriter class directly.

JSchemaValidatingReader

To validate while reading JSON, we made a few changes to the code in figure 9-14. We still use the same JSchema object as the other examples and add the same required fields, but we no longer need to parse a JSON string into a JObject. Instead, we just leave the product JSON as a string and assign it to the prodJson variable. Notice we again leave the required Stock property out of the JSON string, so schema validation will intentionally fail.

Now we have to set up our JSchemaValidatingReader object. The JSchemaValidatingReader constructor does not take a string, it takes a JsonReader derived class. So we must perform a few extra steps to convert our JSON string into a reader. First, we convert the JSON string to a StringReader by passing it to the StringReader constructor. Then we pass the StringReader object to the JsonTextReader constructor. Since JsonTextReader derives from the JsonReader class, we can pass it to the JSchemaValidatingReader constructor.

```
Figure 9-14

public void Go()
{
    //manually generate the schema
    var productSchema = new JSchema
    {
        Type = JSchemaType.Object,
        Properties = {
            { "Name", new JSchema { Type = JSchemaType.String } },
            { "Stock", new JSchema { Type = JSchemaType.Integer } },
            { "Sizes", new JSchema { Type = JSchemaType.Array,
```

```
                        Items =
                        {
                            new JSchema { Type = JSchemaType.String }
                        }
                    }
                }
            }
        };

        //add required properties
        productSchema.Required.Add("Name");
        productSchema.Required.Add("Stock");
        productSchema.Required.Add("Sizes");

        //JSON string
        var prodJson = @"
        {
            ""Name"": ""Shirt"",
            ""Sizes"": [""Medium"", ""Large""],
            ""UPC"": ""123456789""
        }";

        //declare JSchemaValidatingReader
        var reader = new JsonTextReader(new StringReader(prodJson));
        var validatingReader = new JSchemaValidatingReader(reader);
        validatingReader.Schema = productSchema;

        //declare list to catch any error messages
        IList<string> errorsList = new List<string>();
        validatingReader.ValidationEventHandler +=
                            (o, a) => errorsList.Add(a.Message);

        //validate
        var serializer = new JsonSerializer();
        var product = serializer.Deserialize<Product>(validatingReader);

        //get error messages
        var errorMessages = String.Join(";", errorsList.ToArray());
}
```

Now we can set a few properties on our JSchemaValidatingReader object. First we assign the productSchema object to the Schema property, so the validating reader will know which schema to validate against. Then we initialize a list of strings to hold any error messages. To handle any errors, we set the ValidatingEventHandler property to a lambda expression that adds any error messages to the errorsList.

Finally, a JsonSerializer object is instantiated and its Deserializer() method is called, with the JSchemaValidatingReader object passed as a parameter, since it derives from JsonReader.

Since we intentionally caused the validation to fail by omitting the Stock member from the source JSON, the errorMessages variable will contain, as expected: "Required properties are missing from object: Stock. Path '', line 6, position 13".

JSchemaValidatingWriter

To force a failed validation while *writing* JSON takes a little different approach than simply omitting the required fields. This is because, if the JSON is missing a property, the class will just initialize the property with a default value. Therefore, we will introduce another element into the schema by setting the JSchema.ExclusiveMinimum property. In figure 9-15, the code starts by manually generating the schema. But this time, notice we define the Stock element with the ExclusiveMinimum property set to true. We also set the Minimum value to 10. When this schema is used for validation, it will ensure that Stock has a value of 11 or more. If we wanted to include 10 as the minimum acceptable value, we would NOT have set ExclusiveMinimum, but only set the Minimum property.

Next we create a product instance. Notice we initialize the Stock property with a value of 5, which is less than the required minimum defined in the schema. Then we begin the process of writing the JSON by creating a StringWriter to pass to the JsonTextWriter constructor. We create a JSchemaValidatingWriter object called validatingWriter by passing the JsonTextWriter object to the constructor. We then set the Schema property of the validatingWriter object to point to our manually generated schema, named productSchema.

As before, we set up a list to collect any error messages and set the ValidationEventHandler. We then create a JsonSerializer instance and serialize the product object with the validating writer.

```
Figure 9-15

public void Go()
{
    //manually generate the schema
    var productSchema = new JSchema
    {
        Type = JSchemaType.Object,
        Properties =    {
            { "Name", new JSchema { Type = JSchemaType.String } },
            { "Stock", new JSchema {
                    Type = JSchemaType.Integer,
```

```
                    ExclusiveMinimum = true,
                    Minimum = 10
                }
            },
            { "Sizes", new JSchema{
                    Type = JSchemaType.Array,
                    Items = {
                            new JSchema { Type = JSchemaType.String }
                        }
                }
            }
        }
    };

    //create Product object
    var product = new Product
    {
        Name = "Shirt",
        Sizes = new List<string>
        {
            "Large", "Medium"
        },
        Stock = 5
    };

    using (var stringWriter = new StringWriter())
    {
        var writer = new JsonTextWriter(stringWriter);
        writer.Formatting = Formatting.Indented;

        var validatingWriter = new JSchemaValidatingWriter(writer);
        validatingWriter.Schema = productSchema;

        IList<string> errorsList = new List<string>();
        validatingWriter.ValidationEventHandler +=
                      (o, a) => errorsList.Add(a.Message);

        var serializer = new JsonSerializer();
        serializer.Serialize(validatingWriter, product);

        //output
        var isValid = (errorsList.Count == 0);
        var errorMessages = String.Join(";", errorsList.ToArray());
        var prodJson = stringWriter.ToString();
    }
}
```

When we run this code, it will not pass validation, as intended. Therefore, the isValid boolean is set to false because an error message was added to the errorsList collection, making its count 1, and not 0. The errorMessages variable will contain the string: "Integer 5 is less than minimum value of 10".

Let's go back and change the value of the Stock property from 5 to 10. Will this now pass validation? Actually, it will not. Since we set the ExclusiveMinimum, the minimum acceptable value would be 11 or more. The errorMessages variable would then contain a different error message: "Integer 10 equals minimum value of 10 and exclusive minimum is true".

If we go back and initialize the Stock property with a value of 11, then the object would pass schema validation when writing JSON. There would be no error messages in the errorList collection. Its count would be 0, and the isValid boolean would be set to true.

```
{
    "Chapter" : "Ten",
    "Title" : [
                    "Binary JSON",
                    "BsonDataReader",
                    "BsonDataWriter"
              ]
}
```

BSON, pronounced Bee-Sawn, is short for Binary JSON. It is basically binary-encoded JSON-like documents that are not human-readable. BSON is designed to be fast to encode and decode. One of the biggest users of BSON is MongoDB, a document oriented NoSQL database that stores its data in BSON format. If you are interested, the BSON specification can be found at bsonspec.org.

The Newtonsoft.Json.Bson namespace has been moved out of the main dll and into its own package. Therefore, the previous BSON classes BsonReader, BsonWriter and BsobObjectId are all obsolete. The new BSON package must be installed separately with NuGet. Visit the following website for more info: https://www.nuget.org/packages/Newtonsoft.Json.Bson. (For detailed instructions on using NuGet, please see Appendix A.) Open your project in Visual Studio, and then open the command line Package Manager Console and type: Install-Package Newtonsoft.Json.Bson -Version 1.0.1

This creates a packages folder in your project folder (if this is the first NuGet package installed). In the packages folder is a Newtonsoft.Json.Bson.1.0.1 folder. It contains a lib folder of dlls. A reference for the Newtonsoft.Json.Bson.dll has been added to the project's References node.

The packages.config file should now look like figure 10-1.

```
Figure 10-1

<?xml version="1.0" encoding="utf-8"?>
<packages>
  <package id="Newtonsoft.Json" version="10.0.3"
             targetFramework="net452" />
  <package id="Newtonsoft.Json.Bson" version="1.0.1"
             targetFramework="net452" />
</packages>
```

As mentioned previously, the BsonReader and BsonWriter classes are obsolete. The new classes used for BSON conversion are BsonDataWriter and BsonDataReader. Let's talk about how to use these classes.

BsonDataWriter

Let's start by serializing a simple hello world JSON object to BSON using BsonDataWriter, as shown in figure 10-2. Don't forget to add a using directive for: using Newtonsoft.Json.Bson;

In the code, a simple JSON key/value pair for hello world is constructed and assigned to the variable jsonStr. Note that the key name is hello, and the value is world. This will make sense later when we look at the underlying BSON binary structure. The JSON is deserialized to an object. Then we create a MemoryStream that we pass to the BsonDataWriter constructor. We create a JsonSerializer object and serialize the JSON object to the BSON writer. Then we write the BSON data to a file called helloworld.bson.

```
Figure 10-2

public void Go()
{
    var jsonStr = @"{""hello"":""world""}";
    var helloObject = JsonConvert.DeserializeObject(jsonStr);

    using (var bsonStream = new MemoryStream())
    {
        using (var bsonWriter = new BsonDataWriter(bsonStream))
        {
            var jsonSerializer = new JsonSerializer();
            jsonSerializer.Serialize(bsonWriter, helloObject);
            using (var file = new FileStream(@"C:\helloworld.bson",
                FileMode.Create, FileAccess.Write))
            {
                bsonStream.WriteTo(file);
            }
        }

        foreach (byte b in bsonStream.ToArray())
        {
            Console.WriteLine("x" + b.ToString("X2") +
                " -- " + Encoding.ASCII.GetString(new byte[] { b }));
        }
    }
}
```

But before we inspect the contents of helloworld.bson file, let's talk a little about the BSON binary structure. BSON objects consist of an ordered list of elements. Each element contains three items: field type, field name and field value. If the field name and/or field value are strings, they will end with a null terminator, hex value x00. The end of the data is also signaled by hex value x00, which denotes end of object (EOO).

Okay. Now we'll open the helloworld.bson file in Visual Studio to inspect the data. The contents should appear as they do in figure 10-3:

```
Figure 10-3

00000000   16 00 00 00 02 68 65 6C   6C 6F 00 06 00 00 00 77
                                           ...hello.....w
00000010   6F 72 6C 64 00 00                   orld..
```

Each row starts with eight digits representing the address of the first byte of each line. Then come eight sets of numbers, representing hex numbers, followed by eight more hex numbers, for a total of sixteen hex values. The row ends with a visual ASCII representation of the sixteen hex values. Those hex values that don't have a printable representation appear as a period.

Let's take a closer look at the first eight hex numbers. The first 4 bytes of hex numbers (16 00 00 00) hold the total document size of 22 bytes as a 32-bit little-endian integer.

The next hex number (02) is the Field Type. 02 means the value will be a string. A list of other field types appear in figure 10-4.

```
Figure 10-4

x01 = Floating point
x02 = UTF-8 string
x03 = Embedded document
x04 = Array
x05 = Binary data
x06 = Deprecated
x07 = (byte*12) ObjectId
x08 = Boolean "false"
x08 = Boolean "true"
x09 = int64 UTC milliseconds in Unix epoch
x0A = Null value
x0B = Regular expression
x0C = Deprecated
x0D = JavaScript Code
x0E = Symbol
x0F = JavaScript code w/ scope
x10 = 32-bit Integer
x11 = Timestamp.
x12 = 64-bit integer
xFF = Min key
x7F = Max key
```

The next five hex numbers (68 65 6C 6C 6F) represent the five characters in the Field Name. They are hex values for the string "hello". If you recall, in the JSON key/value pairs, the key name was hello.

The next hex number, 00, represents the null terminator for the Field Name.

The next four hex numbers (06 00 00 00) hold the size of the Field Value.

The next five hex numbers (77 6F 72 6C 64) hold the five characters of the Field Value. They are the hex values for the string "world". If you recall, in the JSON key/value pairs, the value was equal to world.

The next hex number, 00, represents the null terminator for the Field Value.

The next hex number, 00, represents the end of object (EOO).

The last part of the program in figure 10-2 loops through the stream and writes the hex values to the console. The output appears in figure 10-5. Notice how the five hex values (68 65 6C 6C 6F) make up the string 'hello' and the five hex values (77 6F 72 6C 64) make up the string 'world'. Some characters could not be represented by the file's character set and were replaced by question marks.

```
Figure 10-5

x16 -- ?
x00 --
x00 --
x00 --
x02 -- ?
x68 -- h
x65 -- e
x6C -- l
x6C -- l
x6F -- o
x00 --
x06 -- ?
x00 --
x00 --
x00 --
x77 -- w
x6F -- o
x72 -- r
x6C -- l
x64 -- d
x00 --
x00 --
```

Now that we have a basic understanding of the BSON format, let's deserialize some BSON to our Product class. The code in figure 10-6 has two methods. Let’s talk about the second method GetProductBsonBase64() because it basically acts as our BSON data source, retuning the BSON data in a base64 string for easy transport.

```
Figure 10-6
public void Go()
{
    var bson64Str = GetProductBsonBase64();
    byte[] bsonData = Convert.FromBase64String(bson64Str);

    //deserialize back to .NET object
    var product = new Product();
    using (var bsonStream = new MemoryStream(bsonData))
    {
        using (var bsonReader = new BsonDataReader(bsonStream))
        {
            var jsonSerializer = new JsonSerializer();
            product =
                  jsonSerializer.Deserialize<Product>(bsonReader);
        }
    }
}
```

```
public string GetProductBsonBase64()
{
    var jsonStr = @"{
        ""Name"": ""Shirt"",
        ""Stock"": ""5"",
        ""Sizes"": [
            ""Large"",
            ""Medium""
        ]
    }";
    var jsonObj = JsonConvert.DeserializeObject(jsonStr);

    using (var bsonStream = new MemoryStream())
    {
        using (var bsonWriter = new BsonDataWriter(bsonStream))
        {
            var jsonSerializer = new JsonSerializer();
            jsonSerializer.Serialize(bsonWriter, jsonObj);
        }
        return Convert.ToBase64String(bsonStream.ToArray());
    }
}
```

The GetProductBsonBase64() method starts by defining a product JSON string and assigning it to the jsonStr variable. Then it is deserialized into an object called jsonObj. A MemoryStream object called bsonStream is then created to hold the binary JSON. The bsonStream is passed to the BsonDataWriter constructor. A JsonSerializer is created which serializes the JSON object to BSON. Next, we convert the binary data in the stream to a base64 string by calling the Convert.ToBase64String() method and return it to the calling method. The base64 string appears in figure 10-7.

Figure 10-7

base64 string
SQAAAAJOYW1lAAYAAABTaGlydAACU3RvY2sAAgAAADUABFNpemVzACAAAAACMAAGAAAA
TGFyZ2UAAjEABwAAAE1lZGl1bQAAAA==

The Go() method in figure 10-6 starts out by calling the GetProductBsonBase64() method and assigning the base64 string to a variable named bson64Str. The base64 string is then converted to a bytes array by calling Convert.FromBase64String(). The bytes array is converted to a stream by passing it to a MemoryStream constructor. A JsonSerializer is created which deserializes the

BSON to a product object. If we were to peek at the contents of the product object, it would resemble the display in figure 10-8.

```
Figure 10-8

product:
    Name        = "Shirt"
    Sizes       = Count = 2
    Stock       = 5
```

{

"Chapter" : "Eleven",

"Title" : "Working with XML"

}

Json.NET can convert XML to JSON using the methods SerializeXmlNode() and DeserializeXmlNode(). Internally, Json.NET converts XML to JSON using a JsonConverter named XmlNodeConverter. If your .NET framework version supports XDocument, then the SerializeXNode() and DeserializeXNode() methods will also be available.

Json.NET will preserve the following XML items when converting to JSON: elements, attributes, text, comments, character data, processing instructions, namespaces and XML declarations.

Things to be aware of when converting XML to JSON, is that any XML attributes will be converted to a JSON property name beginning with an @, and will be inserted as the first item. The XML declaration and processing instructions will be prefixed with ?. Multiple XML nodes with the same name, and at the same level, will be converted to a JSON array (though items may not appear in the same order). Any empty self-closing elements will be converted to null.

SerializeXmlNode()

The code to convert XML to JSON appears in figure 11-1. F or simplicity's sake, we define an XML string in the xml variable. After instantiating an XmlDocument object, we call the LoadXml() method and pass it the xml string. If we instead wanted to load XML direct from a file, we would have used the Load() method and passed it the file path.

There are a few things to notice in the source XML before it gets converted to JSON. The products element has two child product elements, and each product element has an inline pid attribute. And finally, sizes is a self-closing element with no value. We will revisit these items in the converted JSON.

To convert the XML to JSON requires one line of code: a call to the SerializeXmlNode(), passing it the XmlDocument object.

```
Figure 11-1

public void Go()
{
    var xml = @"<?xml version='1.0' standalone='no'?>
    <products>
        <product pid='1'>
            <name>Shirt</name>
            <stock>5</stock>
            <sizes />
        </product>
        <product pid='2'>
            <name>Pants</name>
            <stock>6</stock>
            <sizes />
        </product>
    </products>";

    var doc = new XmlDocument();
    doc.LoadXml(xml);

    var jsonStr =
            JsonConvert.SerializeXmlNode(doc, Formatting.Indented);
}
```

After running this code, the JSON content of the jsonStr variable appears in figure 11-2. It contains two root objects: xml and products. The first object contains the XML declaration information. Notice the name was prepended with a question mark and that both in-line attributes have been turned into key/value pairs with an @ prepended to the name. The second object, the products XML root element, contains the product data. Notice the two child product elements have been converted to an array with two product objects. As expected, the product pid XML attributes have been turned into their own key/value pairs with an @ prepended to the name. And finally, the size values are null, since the original XML elements were empty.

Figure 11-2

```
{
  "?xml": {
    "@version": "1.0",
    "@standalone": "no"
  },
  "products": {
    "product": [
      {
        "@pid": "1",
        "name": "Shirt",
        "stock": "5",
        "sizes": null
      },
      {
        "@pid": "2",
        "name": "Pants",
        "stock": "6",
        "sizes": null
      }
    ]
  }
}
```

Single Item Arrays

As mentioned previously, multiple XML elements with the same name, and on the same level, will be converted into a JSON array. But a problem occurs when the collection in the source contains only a single item, because it will get converted into a single JSON key/value pair instead of a JSON array. To illustrate this issue, we updated our source XML to populate the sizes elements, as shown in figure 11-3. Notice the "Shirt" product now has two XML elements named sizes that contain the values Large and Medium. But the "Pants" product has only one XML element named size that contains the value 33.

```
Figure 11-3

var xml = @"<?xml version='1.0' standalone='no' ?>
<products xmlns:json='http://james.newtonking.com/projects/json'>
    <product pid='1'>
        <name>Shirt</name>
        <stock>5</stock>
        <sizes>Large</sizes>
        <sizes>Medium</sizes>
    </product>
    <product pid='2'>
        <name>Pants</name>
        <stock>6</stock>
        <sizes>33</sizes>
    </product>
</products>";
```

If we ran this new XML source through the SerializeXmlNode() method, it would create the JSON in figure 11-4. Notice that the two sizes elements for "Shirt" were correctly converted into a JSON array containing strings for Large and Medium. However, our "Pants" product, which contained only one sizes element, was converted into a simple key/value pair, when we really wanted a single item array.

```
Figure 11-4

{
  "?xml": {
    "@version": "1.0",
    "@standalone": "no"
  },
  "products": {
    "product": [
      {
        "@pid": "1",
        "name": "Shirt",
        "stock": "5",
        "sizes": [
          "Large",
          "Medium"
        ]
      },
      {
        "@pid": "2",
        "name": "Pants",
        "stock": "6",
        "sizes": "33"
      }
    ]
  }
}
```

How can we instruct Json.NET to convert this single element into an array? By adding a "json:Array" XML attribute to the sizes element of the Pants product, as shown near the end of the code in figure 11-5. But be advised, in order to resolve the "json:" prefix, you must add an XML namespace to a parent element, as we chose to do in the products element. Otherwise, the code will not compile.

```
Figure 11-5

var xml = @"<?xml version='1.0' standalone='no' ?>
<products xmlns:json='http://james.newtonking.com/projects/json'>
    <product pid='1'>
        <name>Shirt</name>
        <stock>5</stock>
        <sizes>Large</sizes>
        <sizes>Medium</sizes>
    </product>
    <product pid='2'>
        <name>Pants</name>
        <stock>6</stock>
        <sizes json:Array='true'>33</sizes>
    </product>
</products>";
```

When this new XML source is run through the SerializeXmlNode() method, it would create the JSON in figure 11-6. Notice that sizes item in the Pants product now correctly appears as a single item array.

```
Figure 11-6
{
  "?xml": {
    "@version": "1.0",
    "@standalone": "no"
  },
  "products": {
    "product": [
      {
        "@pid": "1",
        "name": "Shirt",
        "stock": "5",
        "sizes": [
          "Large",
          "Medium"
        ]
      },
      {
        "@pid": "2",
        "name": "Pants",
        "stock": "6",
        "sizes": [
          "33"
        ]
      }
```

```
    ]
  }
}
```

DeserializeXmlNode()

When converting JSON to XML, the same rules apply. If you want an element to have an attribute, prepend the Key name with @. The XML declaration must be its own object named ?xml, with the key names for version and standalone prepended with @. The JSON source appears in figure 11-7 and is assigned to the jsonStr variable.

Then we simply pass jsonStr to the DeserializeXmlNode() method and it is converted into an XmlDocument object. We select the product's name node and get its InnerText. After this code is run, the productName variable contains the string: Shirt.

```
Figure 11-7

public void Go()
{
    var jsonStr = @"{
            ""?xml"": {
            ""@version"": ""1.0"",
            ""@standalone"": ""no""
        },
        ""products"": {
            ""product"": [
                {
                    ""@pid"": ""1"",
                    ""name"": ""Shirt"",
                    ""stock"": ""5"",
                    ""sizes"": [
                        ""Large"",
                        ""Medium""
                    ]
                },
                {
                    ""@pid"": ""2"",
                    ""name"": ""Pants"",
                    ""stock"": ""6"",
                ""sizes"": [
                        ""33""
                    ]
                }
            ]
        }
    }";
```

```
    XmlDocument doc = JsonConvert.DeserializeXmlNode(jsonStr);
    var node = doc.SelectSingleNode("/products/product/name");
    var productName = node.InnerText;
}
```

If we were to export the XML of the doc object, it would create the XML shown in figure 11-8. And there you have JSON converted to XML.

```
Figure 11-8

<?xml version="1.0" standalone=\no"?>
<products>
  <product pid="1\>"
    <name>Shirt</name>
    <stock>5</stock>
    <sizes>Large</sizes>
    <sizes>Medium</sizes>
  </product>
  <product pid="2">
    <name>Pants</name>
    <stock>6</stock>
    <sizes>33</sizes>
  </product>
</products>
```

DeserializeXNode()

If you have .NET framework 3.5 or later, Json.NET provides a method to deserialize JSON to an XDocument object. XDocument is part of the LINQ to XML API and allows you to query XML using Linq. XDocument also makes it easier to manually create XML.

The code in figure 11-9 uses the same JSON source string as our previous example. But this time, we pass the jsonStr variable to the DeserializeXNode() method instead of the DeserializeXmlNode() method. Consequently, the JSON is converted into an XDocument object, instead of an XmlDocument object.

Don't forget to add a using directive for: using System.Xml.Linq;

```
Figure 11-9

public void Go()
{
    var jsonStr = @"{
            ""?xml"": {
            ""@version"": ""1.0"",
            ""@standalone"": ""no""
        },
        ""products"": {
            ""product"": [
                {
                    ""@pid"": ""1"",
```

```
                    ""name"": ""Shirt"",
                    ""stock"": ""5"",
                    ""sizes"": [
                        ""Large"",
                        ""Medium""
                    ]
                },
                {
                    ""@pid"": ""2"",
                    ""name"": ""Pants"",
                    ""stock"": ""6"",
                    ""sizes"": [
                        ""33""
                    ]
                }
            ]
        }
    }";

    //deserialize back to XML XDocument
    XDocument xdoc = JsonConvert.DeserializeXNode(jsonStr);

    var products = from item in xdoc.Descendants("product")
            select new Product
            {
                Id = (int)item.Attribute("pid"),
                Name = (string)item.Element("name"),
                Sizes = item.Elements("sizes")
                        .Select(p => p.Value).ToList(),
                Stock = (int)item.Element("stock")
            };
}
```

Now we can run a Linq query on the XDocument object to return all the product elements in the XDocument. For each <product> element found, we create a Product instance. To extract values from the pid attributes, we use the Attribute() method. To get values from single elements, like for Name and Stock, we use the Element() method. And for Sizes, we use the Elements() method to get values from the multiple sizes elements.

To accommodate the value from the pid attribute, we had to add an Id property to the Products class, as shown in figure 11-10.

```
Figure 11-10

public class Product
{
    public string Name { get; set; }
    public int Id { get; set; }
    public int Stock { get; set; }
    public List<string> Sizes { get; set; }
}
```

Also notice in figure 11-9, that the XML element names did not exactly match our class property names. For example, the pid attribute value was assigned to Product.Id. This is a good place to handle any custom transformations you may need to make.

If we were to export the XML of the xdoc object, it would create the XML shown in figure 11-11.

```
Figure 11-11

<products>
  <product pid="1">
    <name>Shirt</name>
    <stock>5</stock>
    <sizes>Large</sizes>
    <sizes>Medium</sizes>
  </product>
  <product pid="2">
    <name>Pants</name>
    <stock>6</stock>
    <sizes>33</sizes>
  </product>
</products>
```

DeserializeXNode() Overloads

The DeserializeXNode() method has a couple overloads for added functionality. Passing a string parameter for deserializeRootElementName allows you to change the name of the root element. Passing an additional boolean parameter for writeArrayAttribute will add the "json:Array" attribute so single elements can later be converted as an JSON array. We passed in both parameters to the DeserializeXNode() method as shown in the last line of figure 11-12.

```
Figure 11-12

public void Go()
{
    var jsonStr = @"{
            ""?xml"": {
            ""@version"": ""1.0"",
            ""@standalone"": ""no""
        },
        ""products"": {
            ""product"": [
                {
                    ""@pid"": ""1"",
                    ""name"": ""Shirt"",
                    ""stock"": ""5"",
```

```
                    ""sizes"": [
                        ""Large"",
                        ""Medium""
                    ]
                },
                {
                    ""@pid"": ""2"",
                    ""name"": ""Pants"",
                    ""stock"": ""6"",
                    ""sizes"": [
                        ""33""
                    ]
                }
            ]
        }
    }";

    //deserialize back to XML XDocument
    var xdoc = JsonConvert.DeserializeXNode(jsonStr, "ProductsList",
                    true);
}
```

The XML exported from the XDocument xdoc object appears in figure 11-13. Notice the root element name is now ProductsList instead of products. Also notice the json:Array attribute and corresponding namespace was added to the single sizes XML element for Pants, but not to any of the multiple sizes elements for Shirt.

```
Figure 11-13

<ProductsList>
  <products>
    <product pid="1">
      <name>Shirt</name>
      <stock>5</stock>
      <sizes>Large</sizes>
      <sizes>Medium</sizes>
    </product>
    <product pid="2">
      <name>Pants</name>
      <stock>6</stock>
      <sizes json:Array="true"
             xmlns:json="http://james.newtonking.com/projects/json">
        33
      </sizes>
    </product>
  </products>
</ProductsList>
```

{

"Chapter" : "Twelve",

"Title" : [

"Logging",

"Callbacks",

"Much, Much, More"

]

}

Json.NET can write a message log of the serialization/deserialization process, including any errors, by using the ITraceWriter interface. Json.NET comes with two built-in classes that implement the ITraceWriter interface; MemoryTraceWriter and DiagnosticsTraceWriter. MemoryTraceWriter keeps log messages in memory, while DiagnosticsTraceWriter writes messages to any System.Diagnostics.TraceListeners you may have set up. You can also send messages to external logging frameworks, such as NLog, just by creating your own custom TraceWriter that implements the ITraceWriter interface. Both the MemoryTraceWriter and DiagnosticsTraceWriter classes implement the ITraceWriter interface. All TraceWriter classes and interfaces are defined in the Newtonsoft.Json.Serialization namespace. We will take a look at developing all three TraceWriter options.

To invoke a TraceWriter, it can be assigned to a property of either a JsonSerializerSettings object or a JsonSerializer object. The code in figure 12-1 starts by creating a product JSON string. Next, a MemoryTraceWriter instance is created and then assigned to the TraceWriter property of a JsonSerializerSettings object. When the DeserializeObject() method is called, the TraceWriter gets busy generating messages which are then exported to the log variable.

Make sure you add a using directive for: using Newtonsoft.Json.Serialization;

```
Figure 12-1

public void Go()
{
    var jsonStr = @"{
            ""Name"": ""Shirt"",
            ""Stock"": ""5"",
            ""Sizes"": [
                ""Large"",
                ""Medium""
            ],
            ""UPC"": ""123456789"",
            ""Price"": 19.99
        }";

    var traceWriter = new MemoryTraceWriter();

    var settings = new JsonSerializerSettings()
    {
        TraceWriter = traceWriter
    };

    var prod =
            JsonConvert.DeserializeObject<Product>(json, settings);

    var log = traceWriter.ToString();
}
```

The output of the MemoryTraceWriter is displayed in figure 12-2. Each line begins with a timestamp (most messages are wrapped over multiple lines). The first message is marked "Info" after the timestamp and indicates it started deserializing the Name property. The next two "Info" messages indicate when it started and ended deserializing the Sizes collection. The fourth message, marked "Verbose", indicates its attempt to deserialize UPC, but it did not find a matching class property. The fifth

"Info" message indicates what time it completed deserializing the Product string. The last "Verbose" message helpfully displays the product JSON.

```
Figure 12-2

2018-01-29T16:18:52.235 Info Started deserializing
   ConsoleTestApp.Product. Path 'Name', line 2, position 27.
2018-01-29T16:18:52.265 Info Started deserializing System.
   Collections.Generic.List`1[System.String]. Path 'Sizes',
   line 4, position 30.
2018-01-29T16:18:52.267 Info Finished deserializing System.
   Collections.Generic.List`1[System.String]. Path 'Sizes',
   line 7, position 21.
2018-01-29T16:18:52.268 Verbose Could not find member
   'UPC' on ConsoleTestApp.Product. Path 'UPC', line 8, position 26.
2018-01-29T16:18:52.269 Info Finished deserializing
    ConsoleTestApp.Product. Path '', line 9, position 17.
2018-01-29T16:18:52.269 Verbose Deserialized JSON:
{
  "Name": "Shirt",
  "Stock": 5,
  "Sizes": [
    "Large",
    "Medium"
  ],
  "UPC": "123456789"
}
```

Custom TraceWriter to NLog

If you want to write logs to an existing logging system, such as the popular NLog framework, you can create a custom TraceWriter just by implementing the ITraceWriter interface. The ITraceWriter interface has only a Trace() method to implement and a LevelFilter property, as shown in figure 12-3. Don't forget to add a using directive for: using System.Diagnostics;

This bare-minimum implementation, however, is not very useful. The Trace() method will be called every time Json.NET has a message to log, therefore we will need to add the appropriate code to this method.

```
Figure 12-3

public class TraceWriter : ITraceWriter
{
    public TraceLevel LevelFilter
    {
        get
        {
            throw new NotImplementedException();
        }
    }
```

```
    public void Trace(TraceLevel level, string message, Exception ex)
    {
        throw new NotImplementedException();
    }
}
```

To use NLog, we must first install it using Nuget. With Visual Studio open to a console project, open the Package Manager Console by selecting menu: Tools -> Nuget Package Manager -> Package Manager Console. At the PM> prompt, type: Install-Package NLog

This will add a reference to the NLog.dll to your project. Don't forget to add a using directive for: using NLog;

Now we can go ahead and create a custom TraceWriter class implementing the ITraceWriter interface, as shown in figure 12-4. The first line creates a static instance of the NLog logger. The LevelFilter property is of type TraceLevel, which is a .NET System.Diagnostics enum indicating what kind of message it is: Error, Warning, Info, or Verbose. In the getter of the LevelFilter property, we set all messages to Verbose. We will let the Trace() method itself override the LevelFilter as needed. The Trace() method accepts parameters for TraceLevel, the message string, and an exception object. We pass the message and the TraceLevel to the NLog Log() method. But first, we must convert the TraceLevel enum to an equivalent NLog message type by passing it to the ConvertToNlogLevel() method. Easy-peasy.

Although we didn't make use of the exception parameter in this simple example, we could have always create a LogEventInfo object, which has properties to hold the level, message and exception. Then the LogEventInfo object would be passed to an overloaded Log() method. But now it is time to write code that invokes this custom TraceWriter.

```
Figure 12-4

public class NLogTraceWriter : ITraceWriter
{
    private static readonly Logger Logger =
                                LogManager.GetLogger("NLogTraceWriter");

    public TraceLevel LevelFilter
```

```
    {
        // trace all messages. nlog can handle filtering
        get { return TraceLevel.Verbose; }
    }

    public void Trace(TraceLevel level, string message, Exception ex)
    {
        // log Json.NET message to NLog
        Logger.Log(ConvertToNlogLevel(level), message);
    }

    private LogLevel ConvertToNlogLevel(TraceLevel level)
    {
        switch (level)
        {
            case TraceLevel.Error:
                return LogLevel.Error;
            case TraceLevel.Warning:
                return LogLevel.Warn;
            case TraceLevel.Info:
                return LogLevel.Info;
            case TraceLevel.Off:
                return LogLevel.Off;
            default:
                return LogLevel.Trace;
        }
    }
}
```

The code in figure 12-5 looks a lot like the code in figure 12-1 that runs the default TraceWriter. In fact, the only difference is that instead of instantiating a new MemoryTraceWriter(), the code instantiates a new custom logger class by calling new NLogTraceWriter(). Then we assign it to the JsonSerializerSettings TraceWriter property as before. And that's it.

When we run this code, NLog will write all the appropriate deserialization messages. But wait a minute. How are we going to view the messages? We cannot just call the ToString() method of the nlogTraceWriter object because that will just output the object name. But we can configure NLog to write the log to a file. There are two ways to do this: programmatically or through the app.config.

```
Figure 12-5

public void Go()
{
    var json = @"{
        ""Name"": ""Shirt"",
        ""Stock"": ""5"",
        ""Sizes"": [
            ""Large"",
            ""Medium""
        ],
```

```
        ""UPC"": ""123456789""
    }";

    var nlogTraceWriter = new NLogTraceWriter();

    var settings = new JsonSerializerSettings()
    {
        TraceWriter = nlogTraceWriter
    };

    var prod =
            JsonConvert.DeserializeObject<Product>(json, settings);
}
```

First, we'll take a look at how to configure this through the app.config, as shown in figure 12-6. The first thing we need to add, is an element in the configSections for nlog. This lets us define a custom schema named "nlog" for storing additional settings. The next element, Startup, is there by default.

After Startup, we define our custom schema by adding an nlog element (notice the element tag name matches the name attribute we defined in configSections). The nlog element contains two child elements: targets and rules. The targets element is where we define the target is a file and specify the path and filename. Norice the filename attribute contains ${basedir} which resolves to the directory where the application runs. This means, when we run the application from within Visual Studio, it will resolve to the project's bin/Debug directory. We also prepend the filename with the year, month, and day.

The rules element is where we specify the minimum level of messages to write. Since the enum is a numbered order, specifying Trace, which is the lowest value, will write all messages. The writeTo attribute of the rules element specifies which target to write to. In our case, it specifies the target we named logfile.

```
Figure 12-6

<?xml version="1.0" encoding="utf-8"?>
<configuration>
  <configSections>
    <section name="nlog"
                type="NLog.Config.ConfigSectionHandler, NLog"/>
  </configSections>
  <startup>
    <supportedRuntime version="v4.0"
                              sku=".NETFramework,Version=v4.5"/>
  </startup>
  <nlog xmlns:xsi="http://www.w3.org/2001/XMLSchema-instance">
    <targets>
```

```
    <target name="logfile" xsi:type="File"
        fileName="${basedir}/${date:format=yyyy-MM-dd}-file.log" />
  </targets>
  <rules>
    <logger name="*" minlevel="Trace" writeTo="logfile" />
  </rules>
 </nlog>
</configuration>
```

Run the Go() method again, and this time, a log file will be written to your project's bin/Debug directory. If you open that file, the contents will look similar to that of figure 12-7. This is very similar to the output of the default TraceWriter log messages, except the messages are marked with levels INFO and TRACE.

```
Figure 12-7

2018-01-30 11:14:53.8772|INFO|NLogTraceWriter|Started deserializing
  ConsoleTestApp.Product. Path 'Name', line 2, position 27.
2018-01-30 11:14:53.9172|INFO|NLogTraceWriter|Started deserializing
  System.Collections.Generic.List`1[System.String]. Path 'Sizes',
  line 4, position 30.
2018-01-30 11:14:53.9172|INFO|NLogTraceWriter|Finished deserializing
  System.Collections.Generic.List`1[System.String]. Path 'Sizes',
  line 7, position 21.
2018-01-30 11:14:53.9172|TRACE|NLogTraceWriter| Could
  not find member 'UPC' on ConsoleTestApp.Product. Path 'UPC',
  line 8, position 26.
2018-01-30 11:14:53.9172|INFO|NLogTraceWriter|
  Finished deserializing ConsoleTestApp.Product. Path '',
  line 9, position 17.
2018-01-30 11:14:53.9172|TRACE|NLogTraceWriter|Deserialized JSON:
{
  "Name": "Shirt",
  "Stock": 5,
  "Sizes": [
    "Large",
    "Medium"
  ],
  "UPC": "123456789"
}
```

If you don't want to edit the app.config, you can always set the file configuration programmatically, as we did in figure 12-8. The only change we made was to add an NLogTraceWriter() constructor. In the constructor, a FileTarget instance is created and its FileName property is set to the same file path we used in the app.config. Next, we define our logging rules by passing the appropriate values to an overloaded LoggingRule constructor. Then we create a LoggingConfiguration instance and add the FileTarget and Rules objects previously created. Finally, we assign the config object to the LogManager Configuration property. You can delete all the app.config entries and the file will still be written to the bin/Debug folder.

Don't forget to add using directives for:

using NLog.Config;

using NLog.Targets;

```
Figure 12-8

public class NLogTraceWriter : ITraceWriter
{
    private static readonly Logger Logger =
                          LogManager.GetLogger("NLogTraceWriter");

    public TraceLevel LevelFilter
    {
        // trace all messages. nlog can handle filtering
        get { return TraceLevel.Verbose; }
    }

    public NLogTraceWriter()
    {
        //define file
        var fileTarget = new FileTarget();
        fileTarget.FileName =
                "${basedir}/${date:format=yyyy-MM-dd}-file.log";
        //define logging rules
        var loggingRule = new LoggingRule("*", LogLevel.Trace,
                                          fileTarget);
        //add rules and targets to configuration
        var config = new LoggingConfiguration();
        config.AddTarget("file", fileTarget);
        config.LoggingRules.Add(loggingRule);
        LogManager.Configuration = config;
    }

    public void Trace(TraceLevel level, string message, Exception ex)
    {
        // log Json.NET message to NLog
        Logger.Log(ConvertToNlogLevel(level), message);
    }

    private LogLevel ConvertToNlogLevel(TraceLevel level)
    {
        switch (level)
        {
            case TraceLevel.Error:
                return LogLevel.Error;
            case TraceLevel.Warning:
                return LogLevel.Warn;
            case TraceLevel.Info:
                return LogLevel.Info;
            case TraceLevel.Off:
                return LogLevel.Off;
            default:
```

```
                return LogLevel.Trace;
            }
        }
    }
```

Let's see what kind of logging messages are written when an error occurs. The only code change made in figure 12-9 is adding a MissingMemberHandling property in the JsonSerializerSettings object so it throws an error if any JSON properties are not defined in the deserialization class. If you run this code it will indeed throw an exception during deserialization because there is no UPC property in the Product class. Run the code. The program will end abruptly because of the exception, but a log will still be written.

```
Figure 12-9

public void Go()
{
    var json = @"{
        ""Name"": ""Shirt"",
        ""Stock"": ""5"",
        ""Sizes"": [
            ""Large"",
            ""Medium""
        ],
        ""UPC"": ""123456789""
    }";

    var nlogTraceWriter = new NLogTraceWriter();

    var settings = new JsonSerializerSettings()
    {
        TraceWriter = nlogTraceWriter,
        MissingMemberHandling = MissingMemberHandling.Error
    };

    var prod =
            JsonConvert.DeserializeObject<Product>(json, settings);
}
```

If you open the log file in your bin/Debug folder, you will see results shown in figure 12-10. Notice that the last message was written as an ERROR level message which corresponds with the exception thrown due to the missing UPC property.

```
Figure 12-10

2018-01-30 14:51:52.1851|INFO|NLogTraceWriter|Started deserializing
  ConsoleTestApp.Product. Path 'Name', line 2, position 27.
2018-01-30 14:51:52.2231|INFO|NLogTraceWriter|Started
```

```
  deserializing System.Collections.Generic.List`1[System.String].
  Path 'Sizes', line 4, position 30.
2018-01-30 14:51:52.2271|INFO|NLogTraceWriter|Finished
  deserializing System.Collections.Generic.List`1[System.String].
  Path 'Sizes', line 7, position 21.
2018-01-30 14:51:52.2271|TRACE|NLogTraceWriter|Could not find member
  'UPC' on ConsoleTestApp.Product. Path 'UPC', line 8, position 26.
2018-01-30 14:51:52.2271|ERROR|NLogTraceWriter|Error deserializing
  ConsoleTestApp.Product. Could not find member 'UPC' on object of
  type 'Product'. Path 'UPC', line 8, position 26.
```

DiagnosticsTraceWriter

Finally, let's look at how to use the Json.NET DiagnosticsTraceWriter to write log messages to an existing Trace Listener. A trace listener collects and routes trace messages to the appropriate target. For example, if you wanted to write trace messages to an event log, you would set up an EventLogTraceListener. If you wanted to write trace messages to the console, you would set up a ConsoleTraceListener. If you want to write trace messages to a stream or a text file, you would set up an TextWriterTraceListener. There are other types of listeners, but we will focus on setting up a TextWriterTraceListener.

You can set up a trace listener using the app.config, or programmatically in the C# code. To set up a listener in the app.config, you would insert the code in figure 12-11 inside the <configuration> element.

```
Figure 12-11

<system.diagnostics>
  <trace autoflush="true">
    <listeners>
      <add name="myListener"
           type="System.Diagnostics.TextWriterTraceListener"
           initializeData="TextWriterTraceOutput.log" />
      <remove name="Default" />
    </listeners>
  </trace>
</system.diagnostics>
```

In the <trace> element, we set the autoflush attribute to true. Ordinarily, the listener will not write to file until Trace.Flush() is called. Autoflush eliminates the need to call the Flush() method, which suits the purposes of this demo.

Next, new listeners are added inside the <listeners> element. Each listener is added within an <add> element. The name attribute gives each listener an identifier.

The type attribute specifies what kind of listener to set up, which in our case, is a TextWriterTraceListener. The initializeData attribute is where we specify the file name. If the program is run from inside Visual Studio, the log file will appear in the bin/Debug folder of your application.

Notice we also add a <remove> element. This is needed to delete the Default listener that is automatically added. If we don't, then there will be two listeners configured, one named "myListener" and one named "Default", with each receiving the same trace messages.

The Go() method in figure 12-12 is basically the same as we have always used. It creates a JSON string, except we purposely added a UPC property that is not defined in the deserialization class, just so that it would force some interesting log messages. Then we instantiate the DiagnosticsTraceWriter class. Notice we set the LevelFilter property to Verbose so all level of messages are written to the log file. Next, a JsonSerializerSettings object is created and the DiagnosticsTraceWriter object is assigned to the TraceWriter property. The settings object is then passed to the DeserializeObject() method.

```
Figure 12-12

public void Go()
{
    var jStr = @"{
        ""Name"": ""Shirt"",
        ""Stock"": ""5"",
        ""Sizes"": [
            ""Large"",
            ""Medium""
        ],
        ""UPC"": ""123456789""
    }";

    var diagsTraceWriter = new DiagnosticsTraceWriter();
    diagsTraceWriter.LevelFilter = TraceLevel.Verbose;

    var settings = new JsonSerializerSettings
    {
        TraceWriter = diagsTraceWriter
    };

    var prod =
            JsonConvert.DeserializeObject<Product>(jStr, settings);
}
```

After running the code, open the "TextWriterTraceOutput.log" file in your bin/Debug folder. You should see output similar to the other examples, shown in figure 12-13.

```
Figure 12-13

Newtonsoft.Json Information: 0 : Started deserializing
   ConsoleTestApp.Product. Path 'Name', line 2, position 23.
Newtonsoft.Json Information: 0 : Started deserializing
   System.Collections.Generic.List`1[System.String]. Path 'Sizes',
   line 4, position 26.
Newtonsoft.Json Information: 0 : Finished deserializing
   System.Collections.Generic.List`1[System.String]. Path 'Sizes',
   line 7, position 17.
Newtonsoft.Json Verbose: 0 : Could not find member 'UPC' on
   ConsoleTestApp.Product. Path 'UPC', line 8, position 22.
Newtonsoft.Json Information: 0 : Finished deserializing
   ConsoleTestApp.Product. Path '', line 9, position 13.
Newtonsoft.Json Verbose: 0 : Deserialized JSON:
{
  "Name": "Shirt",
  "Stock": 5,
  "Sizes": [
    "Large",
    "Medium"
  ],
  "UPC": "123456789"
}
```

Now let's create a listener and add it *programmatically*, as shown in figure 12-14 (don't forget to delete the code we added to the app.config). The only thing different is the first four lines of code. The first line clears any existing listeners, in particular, the Default listener. The next line instantiates the TextWriterTraceListener class, passing it the log filename and a name for the listener. The third line adds the new listener to the Trace Listeners collection. Finally, we set the AutoFlush option to true. Alternatively, we could have just added a Trace.Flush() call to the very end of the code to trigger the file write.

And that is it. You would see the same log messages in the resulting log file.

```
Figure 12-14

public void Go()
{
    Trace.Listeners.Clear(); //delete Default listener
    var textTraceListener = new TextWriterTraceListener(
                     "TextWriterTraceOutput.log", "myListener");
    Trace.Listeners.Add(textTraceListener);
    Trace.AutoFlush = true;
```

```
    var jStr = @"{
        ""Name"": ""Shirt"",
        ""Stock"": ""5"",
        ""Sizes"": [
            ""Large"",
            ""Medium""
        ],
        ""UPC"": ""123456789""
    }";

    var diagsTraceWriter = new DiagnosticsTraceWriter();
    diagsTraceWriter.LevelFilter = TraceLevel.Verbose;

    var settings = new JsonSerializerSettings
    {
        TraceWriter = diagsTraceWriter
    };

    var prod =
            JsonConvert.DeserializeObject<Product>(jStr, settings);
}
```

Serialization Callbacks

Json.NET supports serialization callbacks by decorating a method with .NET attributes: OnSerializingAttribute, OnSerializedAttribute, OnDeserializingAttribute, OnDeserializedAttribute. These attributes are not part of Json.NET. They have been around the .NET framework since the XML days. Json.Net callbacks trigger events before or after the serialization/deserialization process and can call methods you define to manipulate .NET objects. Simply decorate the method you want to call with the appropriate attribute.

```
[OnSerializing] use this attribute to decorate the method you want
called prior to serialization.

[OnSerialized] use this attribute to decorate the method you want
called after serialization.

[OnDeserializing] use this attribute to decorate the method you want
called prior to deserialization.

[OnDeserialized] use this attribute to decorate the method you want
called after deserialization.
```

Remember, the callbacks give you a hook to manipulate*.NET objects* during the serialization/deserialization process. You won't have access to JSON properties, but that is okay because you have learned many other ways to customize serialization with converters, serializer settings and attributes.

OnSerializing

Notice in figure 12-15, that we modified the Product class by adding a CapitalizePropertyValue() method. It capitalizes the first letter of the string value for Name, if it is lowercase. We want this method called before the serialization process occurs, so we decorate it with the [OnSerializing] attribute. Don't forget to add a using directive for: using System.Runtime.Serialization;

```
Figure 12-15

public class Product
{
    public string Name { get; set; }
    public int Stock { get; set; }
    public List<string> Sizes { get; set; }

```

```
    [OnSerializing]
    internal void CapitalizePropertyValue(StreamingContext context)
    {
        //capitalize values
        if (!String.IsNullOrEmpty(Name) && char.IsLower(Name[0]))
            Name = char.ToUpper(Name[0]) + Name.Substring(1);
    }
}
```

The Go() method in figure 12-16 is much like we've seen before. It instantiates a simple Product object. Notice we initialize the Name property with all lower case characters. When the SerializeObject() method is called, internally it iterates over any defined OnSerializing callbacks. It will trigger the CapitalizePropertyValue() method, which then capitalizes the first letter of the Name string value. When the CapitalizePropertyValue() method completes, control is then returned back to the SerializeObject() method and the serialization process continues.

```
Figure 12-16

public void Go()
{
    var prodObj = new Product()
    {
        Name = "shirt",
        Stock = -5,
        Sizes = new List<string>() { "Small" }
    };

    var jsonStr = JsonConvert.SerializeObject(prodObj);
}
```

If we were to peek at the prodObj values after serialization, they would appear as shown in figure 12-17. Notice the capital "S" in shirt, a result of calling the CapitalizePropertyValue() method.

```
Figure 12-17

prodObj:
    Name        = "Shirt"
    Stock       = -5
    Sizes       = Count = 1
```

The JSON contained in the jsonStr variable appears in figure 12-18. It, too, displays a capital "S". Wait a minute. Did we have access to the JSON, or not? Well, no, we didn't. What happened is the product object was manipulated by the CapitalizePropertyValue() method BEFORE the serialization occurred. After that,

Json.NET serialized the product object. The fact that the value of the Name property is capitalized in the JSON proves the callback method was run before serialization.

```
Figure 12-18

{
  "Name": "Shirt",
  "Stock": -5,
  "Sizes": [
    "Small"
  ]
}
```

OnSerialized

To demonstrate use of the OnSerialized attribute, we modified the Product class in figure 12-19 by adding a DateTime property for the Processed time. We also added a SetProcessedTime() method that updates the Processed property with the current date and time. We decorated the method with the [OnSerialized] attribute, which means it will be called after serialization is complete.

```
Figure 12-19

public class Product
{
    public string Name { get; set; }
    public int Stock { get; set; }
    public List<string> Sizes { get; set; }
    public DateTime Processed { get; set; }

    [OnSerialized]
    internal void SetProcessedTime(StreamingContext context)
    {
        Processed = DateTime.Now;
    }
}
```

When we call the same Go() method defined in figure 12-16, only the three original properties are initialized. Therefore, the new Processed property we added will be initialized with a default value. When the SerializeObject() method is called, Json.NET serializes the Product object before triggering the SetProcessedTime() method. If we were to peek at the prodObj values after serialization, they would appear as shown in figure 12-20. Notice the Processed property contains a valid date and time, the result of calling the SetProcessedTime() method.

```
Figure 12-20

prodObj:
    Name        = "Shirt"
    Processed  = {1/8/2018 1:08:52 PM}
    Sizes       = Count = 1
    Stock       = -5
```

However, if we were to look at figure 12-21 at the JSON contained in the jsonStr variable, the Processed item contains the default value of "0001-01-01T00:00:00". What happened to current date value? If you recall when using the OnSerialized attribute, the serialization occurs BEFORE the callback method runs. So the Processed property was serialized when it still contained the default value. This is an important distinction in timing between using OnSerializing versus OnSerialized.

```
Figure 12-21

{
  "Name": "shirt",
  "Stock": -5,
  "Sizes": [
    "Small"
  ],
  "Processed": "0001-01-01T00:00:00"
}
```

OnDeserialized

Now let's tackle the OnDeserialized attribute. The Product class has been modified again, as shown in figure 12-22. This time we have added a boolean property named InStock and a SetInStock() method. The method just sets the InStock boolean based on the Stock quantity. We decorated the SetInStock() method with the [OnDeserialized] attribute which means it will be called after deserialization is complete.

```
Figure 12-22

public class Product
{
    public string Name { get; set; }
    public int Stock { get; set; }
    public List<string> Sizes { get; set; }
    public bool InStock { get; set; }
```

```
    [OnDeserialized]
    internal void SetInStock(StreamingContext context)
    {
        if (Stock > 0)
            InStock = true;
    }
}
```

The Go() method in figure 12-23 looks much like the deserialization methods we've seen before. It creates a JSON string and then deserializes it to the Product class.

```
Figure 12-23

public void Go()
{
    var jsonStr = @"{
        ""Name"": ""Shirt"",
        ""Stock"": ""5"",
        ""Sizes"": [
            ""Large"",
            ""Medium""
        ]
    }";

    var newProdObj = JsonConvert.DeserializeObject<Product>(jsonStr);
}
```

When this code is run, the call to DeserializeObject() will first deserialize the JSON string to a Product instance, then trigger the SetInStock() method. Since the deserialization occurs first, the Stock property will contain five when theSetInStock() method runs. Since the Stock value of five is more than zero, the InStock property is set to true. If we were to peek at the newProdObj property after deserialization, it would look like the data in figure 12-24. The fact that the InStock property is true instead of false proves the SetInStock() method was called after deserialization set the Stock property to five.

```
Figure 12-24

newProdObj:
    InStock     = true
    Name        = "Shirt"
    Sizes       = Count = 2
    Stock       = 5
```

OnDeserializing

Finally, we'll take a look at OnDeserializing. The utility of OnDeserializing may arguably be nebulous, which is why we saved it for last. But let's say we obtained a license to sell products from the ACME Apparel Company. We write code to call their API and fetch the product JSON, but discover it has a VendorName property that contains "ACME Apparel Company". Naturally, we want to replace this value with our own store name before inserting the product into our database. In fact, we don't even want to deserialize the VendorName from their JSON, so we're going to decorate the VendorName property in the Product class with the [JsonIgnore] attribute, as shown in figure 12-25. Consequently, whatever their JSON has in the VendorName property will now be completely ignored. We also added a SetVendorName() method to update the VendorName property with our own store name. Then we decorate the method with an [OnDeserializing] attribute so it will be triggered before deserialization.

```
Figure 12-25

public class Product
{
    public string Name { get; set; }
    public int Stock { get; set; }
    public List<string> Sizes { get; set; }
    public bool InStock { get; set; }
    [JsonIgnore]
    public string VendorName { get; set; }

    [OnDeserializing]
    internal void SetVendorName(StreamingContext context)
    {
        VendorName = "My Store";
    }
}
```

The Go() method in figure 12-26 simulates the product JSON string we'd likely receive from the ACME Apparel Company API. Notice that VendorName contains the string "ACME Apparel Company" that we'd like to ignore. The code then calls DeserializeObject() to deserialize the JSON string to a Product instance. Prior to the deserialization process, Json.NET will call the SetVendorName() method which will update the VendorName property of the Product instance with the appropriate value. After that, the deserialization process will continue, ignoring the

VendorName property in the JSON. The product object we send to the UpdateDatabase method will now contain the intended value for VendorName.

```
Figure 12-26

public void Go()
{
    var acmeJson = @"{
        ""Name"": ""Shirt"",
        ""Stock"": ""5"",
        ""Sizes"": [
                ""Large"",
                ""Medium""
            ],
        ""VendorName"": ""ACME Apparel Company""
    }";

    var newProdObj =
                        JsonConvert.DeserializeObject<Product>(acmeJson);
    UpdateDatabase(newProdObj);
}
```

If we were to peek at the newProdObj property after deserialization, it would look like the data in figure 12-27. Notice the VendorName contains "My Store" instead of "ACME Apparel Company". This proves that the VendorName item in the JSON was ignored and set as a result of calling the SetVendorName() method.

```
Figure 12-27

newProdObj:
    InStock     = true
    Name        = "Shirt"
    Sizes       = Count = 2
    Stock       = 5
    VendorName   = "My Store"
```

IContractResolver interface

The IContractResolver interface provides a way to customize how .NET objects are serialized/deserialized *without* decorating classes or properties with attributes. This is handy when dealing with third-party classes that you cannot modify. The DefaultContractResolver class implements the IContractResolver interface and is used to resolve a JsonContract for a given type. You can create custom ContractResolvers by inheriting from the DefaultContractResolver class and overriding its methods.

The AllowSerializeContractResolver class defined in figure 12-28 inherits from DefaultContractResolver. The function of the derived class is to decide which properties of a given class will be serialized to the JSON. The new derived class overrides the CreateProperty() method of the DefaultContractResolver. However, the first thing the overridden CreateProperty() method does is call the base class CreateProperty() method of the DefaultContractResolver class.

Figure 12-28

```
public class AllowSerializeContractResolver : DefaultContractResolver
{
    protected override JsonProperty CreateProperty(MemberInfo member,
                        MemberSerialization memberSerialization)
    {
        var jsonProperty =
                    base.CreateProperty(member, memberSerialization);
        jsonProperty.ShouldSerialize = x =>
        {
            if (jsonProperty.PropertyType.Name.Equals("Int32"))
                return true;
            else
                return false;
        };
        return jsonProperty;
    }
}
```

The overridden CreateProperty() method will be called three times in our example, once for each property defined in the Product class in figure 12-29. (If you wanted to grab all the properties and manipulate them all at once, you might instead override the CreateProperties method.)

```
Figure 12-29

public class Product
{
    public string Name { get; set; }
    public int Stock { get; set; }
    public List<string> Sizes { get; set; }
}
```

Deciding whether a property is serialized to the JSON or not, is controlled by the ShouldSerialize property of the JsonProperty class. In figure 12-28, the ShouldSerialize property requires a predicate that returns either true or false. If the predicate returns true, the property is serialized. If the predicate returns false, the property is not serialized. The lambda expression we assigned to the ShouldSerialize property inspects the property's type. If it is an integer, it will be serialized. All other types will not be serialized. Admittedly, this is not the most useful of test cases but is certainly enough to demonstrate conditional property serialization. It is important to understand that at this point, we are just assigning/storing the method and its logic in the ShouldSerialize property. Later on, it will be executed internally by the ShouldSerializer() method of the JsonSerializerInternalWriter class, after it was called by the JsonSerializerInternalWriter SerializeObject() method.

The Go() method in figure 12-30 creates a Product class instance. Then a JsonSerializerSettings object is created with the ContractResolver property set to a new instance of the AllowSerializeContractResolver class. Next, the settings object is passed to the SerializeObject() method which triggers the CreateProperty() method of our custom ContractResolver.

```
Figure 12-30

public void Go()
{
    Product product = new Product
    {
        Name = "Shirt",
        Sizes = new List<string>() { "Small", "Medium", "Large" },
        Stock = 5
    };

    var settings = new JsonSerializerSettings()
    {
        ContractResolver = new AllowSerializeContractResolver()
    };

    var jsonStr = JsonConvert.SerializeObject(product, settings);
}
```

The JSON string contents of the jsonStr variable appears in figure 12-31. As expected, only the Stock integer property was serialized.

```
Figure 12-31

{
  "Stock": 5
}
```

ISerializationBinder interface

A common problem when serializing with TypeNameHandling (as discussed in chapter three), is that the assembly name and namespace info added to the $type property in the JSON may be completely different from the application that deserializes it. An exception will be thrown if the assembly name and namespace cannot be resolved on the current system. For example, let's consider the JSON in figure 12-32, that was originally generated in an example from chapter three. Notice there are two $type properties, one in the root level and one in the Sizes object. They instruct Json.NET what object type to deserialize to.

Figure 12-32

```
{
  "$type": "JsonNetTest.Product, JsonNetTest",
  "Name": "Shirt",
  "Sizes": {
    "$type": "System.Collections.Generic.List`1[[System.String,
                                             mscorlib]], mscorlib",
    "$values": [
      "Small"
    ]
  },
  "Stock": 0
}
```

Notice the value of the root level $type property contains two string values separated by a comma. The first string consist of the namespace and the class name (this is the full name). The second string value is the partial assembly name (devoid of version and PublicKeyToken information). Where does the assembly name value come from? If you right-click on your project, choose Properties, and click the Application tab on the left side, it is the value in the text box under Assembly Name.

To demonstrate the assembly name problem with using TypeNameHandling, let's create a new console project and name it TestProject (or something other than the "JsonNetTest" in the JSON $type, so that the assembly names will differ). The code in figure 12-33 creates a JSON string with a $type property containing an assembly name and namespace from a different assembly (project). Next, it creates a JsonSerializerSettings object with the TypeNameHandling property defined in expectation that the source JSON can deserialized back to the same object type as the original.

```
Figure 12-33

public void Go()
{
    var jsonStr = @"{
        ""$type"": ""JsonNetTest.Product, JsonNetTest"",
        ""Name"": ""Shirt"",
        ""Sizes"": {
            ""$type"":
                ""System.Collections.Generic.List`1[[System.String,
                mscorlib]], mscorlib"",
            ""$values"": [
                    ""Small""
            ]
        },
        ""Stock"": 0,
        ""Recommendations"": null
    }";

    var settings = new JsonSerializerSettings
    {
        TypeNameHandling = TypeNameHandling.Objects
    };

    var prodObj = JsonConvert.DeserializeObject<Product>(jsonStr,
                        settings);
}
```

Unfortunately, when the DeserializeObject() method is called, an exception will be thrown because the assembly name of JsonNetTest cannot be resolved, much less the namespace of JsonNetTest. Later we will discuss a workaround for handling this issue, but the best-case scenario is not to put the assembly info into the $type property in the first place.

To ensure deserialization under a different application assembly name is successful, sometimes it is desirable to eliminate the assembly name information from the $type property, and just use the class name. But how would we do this? How can we customize the $type information? The answer is to use a custom serialization binder that implements Json.NET's ISerializationBinder interface.

Just to clarify, SerializationBinder is a .NET class used to export object type information (full type name and assembly name of the object) during serialization so that it can be used during deserialization to re-create an object of the desired type. In other words, it is responsible for finding types during serialization and deserialization. SerializationBinder is an abstract base class, so all custom binders must extend this class.

Json.NET supports .NET's SerializationBinder with the ISerializationBinder interface. It contains two methods that must be implemented: BindToName() and BindToType(). The minimum implementation appears in figure 12-34.

Don't forget to add a using directive for: using System.Runtime.Serialization;

```
Figure 12-34

public class MyBinder : ISerializationBinder
{
    //called during deserialization
    public Type BindToType(string assemblyName, string typeName)
    {
        throw new NotImplementedException();
    }

    //called during serialization
    public void BindToName(Type serializedType,
            out string assemblyName, out string typeName)
    {
        throw new NotImplementedException();
    }
}
```

The BindToName() method is called during serialization and is where the assembly name and type name are serialized. It takes three parameters: the type of object to create, the assembly name of the serialized object, and the type name of the serialized object.

The BindToType() method is called during deserialization. It takes just two parameters: the assembly name of the serialized object, and the type name of the serialized object.

Figure 12-35 shows our custom serialization binder. Since our simple example will only do serialization, we only added logic for the BindToName() method. The BindToType() method will be fully implemented in a later example.

```
Figure 12-35

public class MyNameBinder : ISerializationBinder
{
    //called during deserialization
    public Type BindToType(string assemblyName, string typeName)
    {
        throw new NotImplementedException();
    }

    //called during serialization
    public void BindToName(Type serializedType,
            out string assemblyName, out string typeName)
    {
```

```
            assemblyName = null;
            typeName = serializedType.Name;
        }
}
```

The Go() method in figure 12-36 first creates a product instance. Next, a JsonSerializerSettings object is created. The TypeNameHandling property is defined so that any $type properties will be interpreted instead of being serialized to the JSON. We also set the SerializationBinder property to an instance of our custom binder class. When the SerializeObject() method is called, the BindToName() method in figure 12-35 will be triggered. The first thing the BindToName() method does is set the assemblyName info to null. Then it sets typeName to the Name property of serializedType, instead of the FullName property, because FullName would include the namespace.

```
Figure 12-36

public void Go()
{
    var product = new Product
    {
        Name = "Shirt",
        Sizes = new List<string>() { "Small", "Medium", "Large" },
        Stock = 5
    };

    var settings = new JsonSerializerSettings
    {
        TypeNameHandling = TypeNameHandling.Objects,
        SerializationBinder = new MyNameBinder()
    };

    //calls BindToName
    var json = JsonConvert.SerializeObject(product, settings);
}
```

The resulting JSON appears in figure 12-37. Notice the $type property now contains only the Product class name, without namespace, without assembly name.

```
Figure 12-37
{
  "$type": "Product",
  "Name": "Shirt",
  "Stock": 5,
  "Sizes": [
    "Small",
    "Medium",
    "Large"
  ]
}
```

Now let's take a look at how we can use a custom SerializationBinder to workaround the problem of getting strange $type info from third-party JSON that cannot be resolved on your system. The custom binder in figure 12-38 will strip out the assembly name and namespace from the $type property so our application can properly desterilize it. The BindToType() method starts by calling Type.GetType(). If the type is one of .NET built-in types, it will be returned and the function is done. If the type cannot be found, such as the case with custom classes, Type.GetType() will return null. If that occurs, we try to find the custom type by passing in the full class name, including the current namespace, while stripping out the old namespace from the typeName.

```
Figure 12-38

public class MyTypeBinder : ISerializationBinder
{
    //called during deserialization
    public Type BindToType(string assemblyName, string typeName)
    {
        var type = Type.GetType(typeName);
        if (type != null)
            return type;
        var ns = this.GetType().Namespace;
        var tn = typeName.Split('.')[1];
        return Type.GetType($"{ns}.{tn}");
    }

    //called during serialization
    public void BindToName(Type serializedType,
             out string assemblyName, out string typeName)
    {
        throw new NotImplementedException();
    }
}
```

The code in figure 12-39 starts by creating JSON with unknown assembly name and namespace in the $type property. Notice the $type property in Sizes contains the type for Generic List. The serializer will be able to resolve this known .NET type without any help. Next, a JsonSerializerSettings object is created. The TypeNameHandling property is defined so that any $type properties will be interpreted instead of being serialized to the JSON. We also set the SerializationBinder property to an instance of our custom binder class. When the

DeserializeObject() method is called, the BindToType() method from figure 12-38 will be triggered. The BindToType() method will be able to return the correct types for both the custom class and the generic list.

```
Figure 12-39

public void Go()
{
    var jsonStr = @"{
        ""$type"": ""JsonNetTest.Product, JsonNetTest"",
        ""Name"": ""Shirt"",
        ""Sizes"": {
            ""$type"":
                ""System.Collections.Generic.List`1[[System.String,
                  mscorlib]], mscorlib"",
            ""$values"": [
                ""Small""
            ]
        },
        ""Stock"": 0,
        ""Recommendations"": null
    }";

    var settings = new JsonSerializerSettings
    {
        TypeNameHandling = TypeNameHandling.Objects,
        SerializationBinder = new MyTypeBinder()
    };

    //calls BindToType
    var prodObj = JsonConvert.DeserializeObject<Product>(jsonStr,
                                settings);
}
```

The source JSON will successfully be deserialized to the Product class. If we were to hover over the prodObj variable during debug, it would display the data shown in figure 12-40.

```
Figure 12-40

prodObj:
    Name        = "Shirt"
    Sizes       = Count = 1
    Stock       = 0
```

{

"Appendix" : "A",

"Title" : "Installing Json.NET"

}

There are two ways to install Json.NET. You can either go to www.newtonsoft.com and download the zip file, unzip it, and manually add a reference for the Newtonsoft.Json.dll to your Project References.

Or, you can use NuGet.

In Visual Studio, you can open NuGet by right-clicking on your project's References node and selecting "Manage Nuget Packages". Type Json.NET in the search box. Click on Newtonsoft.Json in the results pane. On the right-side pane, click the Install button. This will create a packages folder in your project, where your (.sln) solution file resides. Inside the packages folder, will be a NewtonsoftJson folder which will contains the dlls in the lib folder, one for each framework version it supports. And finally it adds a reference to the Newtonsoft.Json.dll to your Project References node. It also creates a packages.config file in your project folder. This file keeps a list of all the packages installed in your project. Its contents are shown in figure A-1.

```
Figure A-1

<?xml version="1.0" encoding="utf-8"?>
<packages>
  <package id="Newtonsoft.Json"
           version="10.0.3" targetFramework="net452" />
</packages>
```

Some developers prefer using the NuGet command line, a Power Shell based tool called the Package Manager Console. To open the console, go to menu: Tools -> NuGet Package Manager -> Package Manager Console. Depending on your version of Visual Studio, these menu names may be a little different, such as Library Package Manager. The console window will appear in the bottom pane (unless you have customized your layout differently). Click after the "PM>" cursor, type:

Install-Package Newtonsoft.Json

and hit the Enter key.

{

"Title" : "Index"

}

Made in the USA
Monee, IL
04 November 2026

67388641R00108